# Life is a Joke and *God,* Wrote It

Jerry Stanecki

*Aimee!*
*Remember the secret!*
*Always Enjoy the journey!*
*[signature] 10/2*

Spirit Canyon Press

*Life is a Joke and God Wrote It* ©2000 by Jerry Stanecki

FIRST EDITION
Library of Congress Cataloging-in-Publication Data
Stanecki, Jerry.
Life is a Joke and God Wrote It / Jerry Stanecki
ISBN 0-9635129-9-4
stanecki@wwnet.net

Home to Myself used with the kind permission of Melissa Manchester and Carole Bayer Sager ©1973 Manchester, Sager. Arista Records. Rumanian Pickleworks-BMI/Sunbeam-BMI/Five Arts Music-BMI

Front cover design by Junebug Clark, Clark/Moore.com, Michael Souter

Some names of people and places have been changed with respect to safeguarding their anonymity, and to protect the guilty.

Printed in the U.S.A.

For information address  Spirit Canyon Press
                         P.O. Box 121
                         Bloomfield Hills, Michigan
                              48303

# Why This Book?

*The humor in the title is to remind us that we are put on earth to enjoy the journey, to celebrate life.*

*Life is a Joke and God Wrote It* comes from a realization that no matter how hard life seems to be, in truth, it never has to be that difficult.

Life is meant to be lighthearted, fun—to be enjoyed. It took me a long time to understand that—in fact, it almost took dying before I got the message.

This book is a true story. One of an investigative reporter, who charged headfirst into mayhem, murder, the mob, teamsters, terrorists, riots…everyday life. Oh, and let's not forget my addiction to alcohol. That was my toughest battle.

It's the story of discovery and recovery and of a most wonderful and powerful gift received.

Spiritual growth comes from the positive reinforcement given when people share their experiences, strengths and hopes.

This is a book about people who had the courage to struggle, to achieve; "winners" who learned how to celebrate life, not just survive it. Hopefully their thought-provoking, real life stories offer you a way to *walk in their shoes* and maybe change your life.

It is in that spirit, I share with you what's been given to me.

ço

# Dedication

*I lovingly dedicate this book to my children.*

Jason Francis Gerald Charles Stanecki

Jeremy James Alexander Stanecki

Anastasia Nora Lee Stanecki

My gift to you is the positive change in me.

The gift to your children is how you live to create "your healthy life pictures" for them.

Love always,

# Acknowledgments

Quantity, it seems, is what most people strive for. For me it's quality. Sometimes, I get to feeling a little sorry for myself, thinking, "Gee, I don't have many friends." Then I realize the quality of the people in my life, who are pure and wonderful gifts.

With that thought in mind, I say thank you to a few of the friends who were so instrumental in my journey to bring this message to you.

My family, especially my lovely daughter, Annie—or Anastasia—as she prefers to be called today. Not a day goes by when she doesn't challenge, support and encourage "her daddy" to push further into the unknown for answers.

My sons, Jason and Jeremy, and Lynda my daughter-in-law, for always being supportive. To Heather, Shayna and Dylan Stanecki, my beautiful grandchildren for making me their hero.

To Carolyn, the mother of our children, thanks for your kind words of support and years of love.

To Junebug Clark, whose humor, great deal of help and warmth of friendship is only exceeded by his talent as an artist and photographer. He is a very special gift in my world.

Neal Shine, who is part leprechaun, part warrior, part poet, and mentor to many. Thank you for your help and guidance.

Mike Mathews, a brother-in-arms, for his guidance into the confusing and challenging world of publishing. Thank you.

To my pals, Tim and Dutch, for listening…and for always offering encouragement and support.

Thanks to Jim Cash, a *Top Gun* writer, who always encouraged and left us all way too soon. You're missed, Jim.

To John Manis, who for thirty-five years has accepted me for who I am, and has always "been there" for me. John, you saved my life more than once.

Thanks to Mark Gantner, a good friend and a great advisor.

Thank you to Michael Souter for his creativity and patience.

To Bill W. and Dr. Bob for the light.

A special thank you to my dear friend, Denise Tawyea, for continued encouragement, inexhaustible energy, unbending support and for just plain "caring." Without you, this book would have been a longer time in coming.

Finally, to each of you, who have shared your feelings, intimate thoughts and secrets, comments, letters and e-mails about how my writing has affected you—that's what I write for—you are appreciated.

*

"I know what I want on my tombstone,"
the old man said to me, then he smiled.

"I spent so much time tuning my harp—
that I never sang the songs I came to sing."

Marshall Fredricks, Sculptor
The most humble man I've ever met.

# Contents

Dear Friends,

I've included a few blank pages like this one throughout the book. Please use them for your thoughts.

# My Name is Jerry

*Several people have asked me what I was feeling during the years of craziness and insanity. Neal Shine, a mentor of mine, and I were having lunch and discussing this topic when the answer came to me. "A good way to describe those years," I said to Neal, "is that I was always on auto-maniac pilot."*

More than a dozen years have passed since I uttered the words admitting I was an alcoholic. Saying them wasn't easy, even though I'd known it for a long time. What I didn't know was that drinking had nothing to do with my problem—it was my thinking.

Alcoholism is not a drinking problem, it's a thinking problem. Addiction is a thinking disease. Anytime some thing or some person controls your free will, it is a thinking problem. Be it alcohol, drugs, work, sex, food, shopping, relationships, fear itself—all are thinking problems.

As a boy, when my friend Bobby Potter asked me what I was going to be when I grew up, I sure didn't say, "Oh, I'm gonna be an alcoholic. I'm gonna work as hard as I can to be an alcoholic."

Accepting and understanding that my alcoholism wasn't by choice freed me from feeling shame for having the disease.

It took me a long time to accept that—my thinking, helped by a lot of alcohol, fear, drugs, anger, and the plain fact that no one had ever taught me how to take care of myself—had cost me a very lucrative career . . . and a lot more.

However, as you will come to understand, alcoholism has also brought me incredible gifts.

When I decided to write about the journey, Neal Shine, the former publisher of the *Detroit Free Press*, suggested telling folks about the old Jerry and what he went through to earn his credentials to speak about spirituality and celebrating life.

The following story of The Newshawk is a humble attempt to share that with you without being self indulgent.

The power—the clarity of the message coming from me—is not from me. It is from a power much greater than I.

I am just the reporter.

છ

# The Newshawk

*For years I was the people's warrior, fighting battles against injustice, corruption and man's abuse of man. As an investigative reporter and consumer advocate whom you watched on television, I worked relentlessly to make the world a better place.*

It was only when my world fell apart that I realized the real war was going on inside of me.

This is the story of the reporter who, driven by despair, pain and failure, turned his investigative skills inward to focus on self. It will give you an intimate look at the battle fought against the demons as they charged, screaming like banshees—their only mission to destroy me.

Like many people, I'd gotten lost when it came to being joyous, happy and free. Lost to a point near total hopelessness.

Strange how life works.

✦ ✦ ✦

In August 1987, a longtime friend had come to town after a stint at a drug-alcohol treatment center in Hawaii. As we sat in my living room, Brannon talked excitedly about what he had learned. I listened carefully because of the pain I was in. My life was not good. A lot had happened to me in a relatively short period of time and I was depressed, bored and drinking too much.

Brannon suggested I try going to an Alcoholics Anonymous meeting.

"If I do that," I said, "the newspaper gossip columns will run with it, and people will think I was fired because I'm a drunk."

But, I had been fired.

3

After fourteen years of hard work, I was no longer wanted by WXYZ in Detroit. Working without a contract for six months, I decided to take a vacation. The day before I left, I went to the news director and asked if he was satisfied with my work. He told me "everything is great."

When I returned from Europe, one of the first things I saw in the pile of mail at home was a letter from Channel 7. It said they no longer needed my services . . . effective immediately.

The words "everything is great" flashed in my mind and the bile in my stomach flared. The letter was dated the day after the news director assured me things were terrific. Show business.

A couple of days later, I went to see the vice president/general manager of Channel 7 about the dismissal. I told him I understood business was business, but since I had given my all for fourteen years, would severance pay be possible.

He didn't take two seconds to think about it.

"We have no moral obligation," he said coldly.

"I hope you never have to experience the feelings I'm having right now," I told him, "I wouldn't wish that on even you." I turned my back on him and walked out the door.

"More coffee?" Brannon asked, bringing me from the past back to the present.

"Huh?"

"More coffee, do you have any more coffee?"

I refilled his cup and handed it to him. Brannon, in turn, handed me a book. A dark blue book with the title almost invisible. It was the Book of Alcoholics Anonymous. It's called the Big Book.

Opening the book without purpose—I found meaning.

Stunned, I stared at the words on the page I had randomly opened the book to.

There, on page 251 of the third edition of the Big Book, was the story called THE NEWS HAWK. It's the story of a reporter who had fought and won a battle with the bottle.

What shocked me was that for years I had been known as "The Newshawk" on Detroit television.

Standing there, reading the words, I wondered how my story had gotten into this book. After a few minutes, I came to my senses and realized the story in the book had been written before I was born.

The Newshawk . . . Big Book . . . coincidence?

No, the story in the book wasn't my story, but it was about me and so many others dealing with addiction.

My life as The Newshawk was one of nailing the bad guys, of righting wrongs, of chasing crooks down the street with camera rolling, banging on ego-driven insensitive bureaucrats. It was a perfect job for me and I was good at it.

I was a Viking charging into battle. There was no challenge too big. Fact is, I was killing myself.

My career as The Newshawk began in 1976 when the news director of WXYZ-TV Channel 7 came to me while I was working at WXYZ radio. Phil Nye asked me if I wanted to do a new consumer feature Channel 7 was developing. The Newshawk, he said, would do stories to help consumers.

I told him if his idea meant doing stories like, is a "Quarter Pounder" a quarter-pound, then I wasn't interested.

"No," he said, "we mean business."

"And management will back me when sponsors threaten to cancel advertising?"

"Yes," he assured me.

"OK, I'll hold you to it," I said.

The job of Newshawk was a natural for me.

I had been raised to believe that if I was a good person and took care of everybody else's needs and problems, I would automatically be happy. After all, that's the way the books read, what the TV shows showed, and movies promised. In reality I was depressed and miserable. I had no idea how to take care of *me*.

## The Early Years

Born insatiably curious, my career as an investigative reporter began when I was just four years old in the Bay View section on the south side of Milwaukee, Wisconsin.

One crisp autumn morning, I was out early looking for action. I spotted a big gray squirrel on Mrs. Sheffler's lawn and ran after it. I was intrigued at how the squirrel was able to run up the giant elm tree like it did and stop—just stop, maybe six feet above my head.

I stood flat against the tree looking straight up at the squirrel, who was making all kinds of excited chuckling noises. My investigation ended when the squirrel promptly put me on the receiving end of my first commentary. The squirrel peed on my head.

Was that a sign of what was still to come for me? Let me just say, as a journalist, there were many times over the years when I heard "piss on you."

Growing up on the south side of Milwaukee on Swain Court was terrific. Swain Court—great name, huh? I was about ten when I looked up the street name in the dictionary. "Swain—male admirer, a lover." I thought that a perfect fit for my romantic nature.

My parents were wonderful, loving people of strong moral standards who believed in working hard. They survived the Great Depression but lost everything they had. As a result, the experience left emotional scars on my family, a family that was not a big fan of trust.

My parents were not drinkers. However, their parents—my grandparents—all were alcoholic drinkers. As a result my parents were alcoholic *thinkers*. That's the only way they were taught to think.

My father, Alexander, was a respected pharmacist who owned a drugstore on the corner of Kinnikinnic and Ohio streets. In those days, when you were feeling poorly, you'd go to the corner drugstore for medical advice before heading for the doctor. Legend is that my father saved a lot of money in doctor bills for folks a bit short of the buck. Dad was a caring man who gave a lot to strangers. But, because of his work, then sickness, Dad was somewhat emotionally absent from my life.

I hung around the drugstore a lot. I was a real people person and loved doing things for others. At four years old I was selling penny candy. By five, I was crawling on top of the ice cream cooler behind the soda fountain so I could reach the cherry, chocolate and vanilla syrup dispensers to make sodas and malts. Sometimes, when I try, I can still see my Dad smiling approval at me from the prescription room as he mixed medicines and I poured sodas.

Gerri, my mom, was the ultimate "controller." At 5'3" she was a loving, caring woman who sadly carried some deep wounds. She felt that she had to control everybody and everything.

As a child, Mom never knew safety—never knew how it felt to be protected. My mother was abandoned by her birth parents and then again by her adoptive mother. She struggled with shame from her childhood experience, shame that cut deeply into her self-esteem.

As I grew older, Mom talked a lot about what seemed to be a favorite story, *The Little Match Girl.* It was a powerful, pitiful, moving tale of a little girl whose parents had died. The child lived alone in the forest.

In the cold of winter she managed to survive by selling matches she bought for a penny and sold for two pennies.

One day no one would buy her matches. It happened again the next day. It was cold, very cold, and the little match girl, with no wood for a fire, lit each match, one at a time, to keep warm.

Each time she'd light a match she'd have a vision of home, of being loved and safe.

The first match burned quickly and, as it did, her vision of a beautiful warm room faded and disappeared as the match burned out.

She struck another match and its blue flame brought a wonderful scene of a beautifully decorated Christmas tree in a warm home.

The little match girl looked up the giant trunk of the Christmas tree, and saw the heavens and a shooting star.

She remembered her mother telling her that when a shooting star appears a soul dies.

Out of nowhere, the girl's grandmother appeared and drew the child to her breast, comforting her, warming her. The little match girl was happy and content.

Suddenly, the grandmother began to fade and the child struck more and more matches trying to keep her grandmother with her. With all her matches gone, the child and her grandmother rose into the sky.

In the morning, the little match girl was found between two houses in the village.

She was dead.

I didn't understand the depth of the effect that story had on my mother until a few years ago. That's when I realized that somehow, that lonely empty hole in Mom's soul seemed to be passed on to me.

Mom worked at Stanecki Pharmacy, and in her spare time, was president of the druggists women's association. She also worked for charity and the war effort. She was an American Red Cross Gray Lady, a nurse's aide.

How handsome she looked dressed in her Gray Lady uniform. I remember seeing her stepping down the two stairs of the No.16 bright orange electric streetcar wearing her uniform and hat with the red cross on it. She looked proud and I felt proud of her.

Those were wonderful years, with lots of exciting things happening around me. They were the years of Victory gardens and scrap metal drives, of horse apples in the street and of the rag man making his rounds in a horse drawn wagon singing, in a high pitched, cracking voice, "Rags—you got rags for me today?"

The world was at war, but I felt safe in the innocence of being a loved child.

✦ ✦ ✦

I attended the first grade at Sacred Heart, a Catholic school where I didn't seem to fit. Restless, bored a lot of the time, I didn't care much for the slow pace of school.

I think part of the problem was that I started school when I was just four years old. Born in January, I was able to start school the September before my fifth birthday.

I was bored with school, but learning a sense of community kept me busy. One of my biggest lessons in community came from the class bully.

Time and time again, "Fat" Sittman pushed his weight and mental terror around the school yard and neighborhood. He was unyielding in his chosen career as bully and enforcer, reigning terror on the innocent, weaker and smaller kids, of which I was one.

One morning, I'd had enough.

Fat, who was twice my size, shoved me down. It was that shove that pushed me over the edge. As I fell, I hit my head on the cement hard enough to see stars and black out. Waking up, I flipped out, jumped up, and somehow managed to knock an unsuspecting laughing "Fat Boy" to the sidewalk. A stunned look on Fat's face turned to terror as I pounced on him and with all my might pounded the living hell out of him.

Screeching like an angry crow, Sister Mary Agnes came charging out of the school. She tugged at me until she managed to pull me off. All the time I was banging Fat's head on the sidewalk.

So impressed—or maybe so terrorized—by my craziness, Thomas "Fat" Sittman, from that day on, became my protector, my buddy, my pal. That night I slept like a baby. I felt empowered.

Sacred Heart didn't have a football team so for the 7th and 8th grade I transferred to Immaculate Conception to play football.

At 4'9" and 86 pounds I wasn't much of a threat. I played running back and defensive back and loved the game. Although not the best player, I was one of the most determined and fearless players on the team.

One scrimmage I charged a 150-pound lineman who was guarding the quarterback. In the collision, the cleat on his football shoes cut into my shin. The next play, with blood streaming down my leg, I charged the big lineman again. Play after play I slammed into him trying to nail the quarterback, my leg covered with torn flesh and blood mixed with dirt.

At the end of practice he walked up to me and said, "you got a lot of guts, Jerry. You're OK."

As he walked away I felt great. I felt accepted.

I was five feet tall during my first year at Bay View High School and all the girls said I was "cute." Because of my early start in school, my classmates were about two years older and a lot bigger than me. The combination of age and size made me real insecure. I was a funny kid and being funny got attention.

My classmates—sometimes even my teachers—seemed to enjoy my sense of humor. Their attention made me feel good because it translated to acceptance, which meant I was liked. Yet at times, I think being funny increased my anxiety as I worried that they might not laugh. Crazy, huh?

I was outgoing, yet inside I was terrified. Never afraid to say what was on my mind, I was afraid of not being accepted, yet felt that if people didn't like me, then "screw them."

I heard an expression that probably says it better. I was like an "Egomaniac with an inferiority complex."

I worked hard at being liked, at being accepted, yet I always felt alone and apart from the other kids. I wanted to be liked. I needed to be liked—desperately needed it—and I was liked. The problem was me. I never believed or trusted that people's feelings for me were sincere and genuine.

At college I studied pre-medicine, planning to be what my parents wanted—a doctor. "What my parents wanted"—anybody relate?

Pre-Med lasted a year or so before I quit. As a joke, I told people the reason I quit was because I couldn't go through life as a Republican.

The real reason I didn't become a doctor was medicine took too long with the books before you got to the action. I needed action; I was a young man in a hurry, always riding the edge.

With my medical career history, I stayed in school part-time and turned to the world of radio. I became a Disc Jockey.

In 1961, I walked into radio station WBON-FM in Milwaukee and talked my way into an audition. The owner of the station liked what he heard and gave me a job. There was one slight hitch—no pay. I worked free for the first six months, but I was "on the air"; I was "Jerry Fontaine," Disc Jockey.

I can't remember why I chose the name Fontaine. All I remember is there was a comedian on television named Frank Fontaine who always played a happy drunk. Ironic?

In those days FM was hardly heard of—for that matter, it was hardly heard. Maybe a couple of hundred people in the listening area had AM/FM radios, and probably half of them didn't know how to find FM.

After about a year of radio "stardom," I came down with a case of the draft-time blues. It was 1964 and mandatory military service was in force; I was facing a "We Want You" letter from Uncle Sam. Not wanting to wait, I volunteered for military service.

Basic training was hard work, but fun. Because of my ROTC college experience I was made a recruit platoon leader, which immediately created resentment among the other guys.

That resentment really didn't bother me much because the job got me a semi-private room.

Another reason I wasn't that troubled was because it was just another part of what had become accepted routine in my mind. I always felt like people didn't care much for me.

Tough training, long hours, plenty of discipline and maximum exposure to a structured way of life were all benefits of being in the Army. It was an interesting time of lessons learned, good and bad.

Basic finished, and it was time for evaluation for my next assignment. "Aha," the burly sergeant said, "radio experience."

With that declaration, he checked a box on the form in front of him. That stroke of the pen put me back in radio—the Army's version of radio—I was sent to Morse code school for 15 nightmarish weeks.

I survived on the hope that after Morse code school I would go to some exotic assignment in Europe. I was such a dreamer in those days.

All my friends drew assignments to places like Switzerland and Germany. Me? My luck stayed consistently bad and I was assigned as an artillery radio operator at Fort Benning, Georgia.

As I think back to those military years, I realize a power greater than me was watching over my life. For example, when my unit was assigned to Vietnam, I had three months left of my tour of duty. I applied for an early release to return to college. If I had not gotten the approval I would have been extended for another year and that year would have been in combat.

At the time I figured the timing of the early release was just luck. I know now, it was much more than luck.

After being honorably discharged (with a Good Conduct medal—much to the chagrin of numerous officers) from the Army, I stayed in Columbus, Georgia. Going to college part-time, I was also working in television and radio.

One night, at WRBL Radio while hosting a music show, I was on my knees looking for an album when *she* walked into the studio.

Carolyn Rose McGee, a stunningly beautiful woman, smiled and said "hello" and I fell in love. Carolyn, a singer, also worked at the station as a television copywriter.

Within a year we were married and our first son, Jason, was born in Columbus on October 20, 1964. Life was good.

✦ ✦ ✦

There was one incident that comes to mind that just might have something to do with addictive thinking and behavior. I say that with tongue in cheek because it's pretty clear now that what happened was a real sign of problems with booze.

In 1964, I was hosting one of the first radio telephone call-in shows in the country on WRBL-AM. The show was well-received and the audience loved me "telling it like it was."

The boss said that me being a man who usually said what was on his mind, especially if he thought there was an injustice involved, made the show edgy. Little did he know.

One evening a couple of hours before the show, I was feeling uneasy and couldn't figure out why, so I drank a couple of martinis to settle down. Let me tell you, settled I wasn't. By the time I got to the studio and took the second telephone call I was roaring. The first caller had hung up.

Talk radio of the 1960's was about to get "really edgy."

The call was from a high school teacher complaining about the school administration. Being a man with a hair trigger, and having all the "logical" answers, I spiked the punch and called for a revolution against the Columbus, Georgia school administration.

Management quickly pulled the plug, sending me to the shower without any applause.

The next day was a day of excuses. From being overtired to overworked, I covered every excuse in the book, but never, not once, did I think that the booze might have had something to do with my thinking, and consequently, my actions.

Life went on—the denial grew deeper.

After about a year of living in Columbus, I started to have strong feelings of impending doom about my father, who'd had a severe heart attack a few years before.

"Carolyn," I said one day, "we need to move to Milwaukee soon, because if we don't, my father will never see my firstborn son."

Being a stand up woman, Carolyn quit her job without complaining. We packed a U-Haul trailer with all that we owned, and loaded a powder blue 1955 Mercury with our belongings. With our son, Jason, perched on top of the pile in the back seat, and dog Dutchess we headed to Milwaukee. The year was 1965.

I remember the first time my father held his grandson. Dad was sitting in an easy chair in our rented lower flat. Arms outstretched, he was holding up my son. Both Dad and Jason were grinning. So proud Dad was—so proud I was.

The moment changed and darkened for me when I saw past the smile and realized that behind it there was pain in my father's face. I felt afraid. What scared me was his color. His face was gray, ashen gray. I saw that as a pre-death pallor.

A few months after that, at 5:10 on the morning of November 10, 1965, my father woke for the last time. He started coughing, couldn't catch his breath and fell across the bed. He was 56 years old. I miss him a lot.

For the next few years I hosted a nightly music show on Milwaukee's WISN Radio—50,000 watts of "Beautiful Music" beamed to the Midwest.

In my third year at WISN, tired of low pay, I and several other jocks joined AFTRA (American Federation of Radio and Television Artists).

The Hearst Corporation, which owned the station, didn't care much for unions; in fact it was notorious for its anti-union position. In what seemed like no time, two of us were on the street and out of work.

✦ ✦ ✦

In 1968, a break came with a job in Oklahoma City. I worked at KTOK Radio for about six months before the owner decided I wasn't working out. He said he couldn't control me.

Another three months passed as I scratched out a living doing commercials and freelance work. They were desperate times. Broke, two kids now, and a new car payment due—our first new car—we were down.

My birthday brought a special gift. I was hired by Lee Allen Smith to work at WKY Radio in the News Department.

As an investigative reporter for WKY Radio, I was relentless. If there was an injustice or a wrong, I was on it.

My work resulted in helping the then Governor of Oklahoma into an all-expense paid vacation to prison. He was convicted of corruption while in office.

While investigating the Oklahoma juvenile justice system, my stories brought radical change. Because of my work, a 14-year-old boy was taken out of the state penitentiary and assigned to a juvenile facility where he would be helped instead of raped.

The famous American Indian Movement Wounded Knee standoff had ended in South Dakota and AIM had moved into a secret camp near Pawnee, Oklahoma.

While authorities searched for the AIM hidden camp, I headed for it. A source of mine close to Russell Means, one of AIM's leaders, had made arrangements for me to meet Means.

It was a hot day—90 degrees plus. Alone in the car, I turned onto an unmarked dirt road in northern Oklahoma. Suddenly, from nowhere, a giant with a shotgun appeared. Startled, I slammed on the brakes. Standing over six feet tall, the Indian was a good 300 pounds. He was big enough to block the sun as he moved to the driver's side of the car. Eyes adjusting to the shadow the Indian cast, I saw a badly pockmarked face, which I thought probably didn't help his self-esteem. He had a very scary attitude.

"Where you goin'?" He demanded, moving the shotgun to within a foot of my face.

"Get that fucking gun out of my face or you're gonna need help." I said quietly, as menacing as I could. I was angry and, as I later realized, dangerously stupid.

He looked surprised but before he had time to really understand what had happened, I said, "I'm here to see Russell Means. He's expecting me."

"We'll see."

Again from nowhere another Indian, armed to the teeth, who could have been the first Indian's twin, came from behind the car and led me up the road.

The tension eased when Russell Means welcomed me warmly. I did the interview with law enforcement helicopters overhead searching for us, I filed radio news reports telling the AIM story.

The day after I got back to the radio station in Oklahoma City, I found myself in a head-to-head confrontation with the FBI. They wanted information I had not broadcast, which was unacceptable to me. I was a journalist, not an FBI agent. If I gave the information to the FBI I would compromise myself and those on the opposite side of the FBI would no longer trust me to tell their side of the story.

I refused to cooperate and the standoff between the FBI and myself was on. I suspect it was a move that sent page one of what's become a many page FBI file on me into type.

Added to the tension, Norm Bagwell, the vice president and general manager of WKY television/radio, was a former FBI agent. I expected the worst, figuring Bagwell, being loyal to his former employer, would find a way to fire me for not cooperating.

Surprisingly, I didn't get fired. I gave Norm Bagwell a lot of credit for standing behind my integrity. I also think national newspaper columnist Jack Anderson helped keep the ax from falling with his story about "A lone Oklahoma newsman taking a stand against the FBI."

From exposing political corruption to fighting crazy judges who put kids in prison, the Oklahoma years were rock and roll years of nonstop action. From standing in a burning state prison at McAlester, Oklahoma, crying from the tear gas, surrounded by violence, to broadcasting live warnings as I watched the terrifying movement of a tornado move destructively through neighborhoods. From rock festivals to covering mad bombers, I moved steadfastly closer to the dark side.

Halloween night 1973, in Detroit, Michigan. A violent thunderstorm raked the metro area. The news director of WXYZ Radio, an ABC Network owned station, offered me a job as reporter and I accepted. We celebrated with dinner and drinks and drinks and—

Just after ten that night, I caught the last flight to Milwaukee to visit my mother for a day before returning to Oklahoma City to sell the house and pack. The plane almost crashed as it made a sideways landing at Grand Rapids in the storm. We still had Lake Michigan to fly over. I ordered another martini and wondered if the storm was an indication of what was to come in Motown. Little did I know . . .

From the 1950s until long after he died, Jimmy Hoffa was one of the most recognized names in North America. He was president of the Teamsters Union, and its two million members did what Hoffa wanted. Jimmy Hoffa had his problems with the U.S. Government, fellow Teamsters who, Hoffa said, "betrayed" him, prison and finally a mysterious ending.

Jimmy was on a "do or die" mission to regain the presidency of the union when one day in July, 1975, he mysteriously disappeared.

## Spring 1974

It was a particularly slow news day, and one of the Detroit newspapers had carried a story about Jimmy Hoffa's wife, Josephine.

The story said Josephine was being forced out as a member of the Teamsters women's auxiliary. The article quoted Jimmy Hoffa and I wondered if the statement in the newspaper was true. I decided to call Jimmy Hoffa.

A couple of phone calls later and I had tracked Hoffa down at his condo in Florida. The problem was Hoffa's telephone number was unlisted. I called the manager of the condo complex and asked her if she would be kind enough to go up to Hoffa's condo and knock on Jimmy's door and ask him to call Jerry Stanecki collect.

"Sure," she said and hung up.

About twenty minutes later the phone rang.

"XYZ News, Stanecki."

"This is Jimmy Hoffa, who the hell are you and what do you want?"

I was caught by surprise with the quickness of his call and by Hoffa's hello, but I managed to shoot back. "I'm the man who wants to know if you said what you said."

"What the hell do you mean?"

I read Jimmy the article in the paper, including quotes attributed to him.

"I never said no such a God damn thing."

"Good, I've got a tape rolling for possible broadcast so you can tell me what you do have to say about this, and I'll put it on the air." He did.

That phone call prompted Jimmy to start checking me out. In the weeks that followed, I got a couple of calls from sources telling me Jimmy Hoffa was asking a lot of questions about me. About a month after my first meeting with Hoffa, I started getting telephone calls from people who didn't care to leave names, but did tell me some fascinating things about "news stories" that had just happened or were about to happen.

"That was some explosion, huh, Jerry?" the gravely voice on the phone asked. "It blew Dave Johnson's boat right out of the water."

I always expected the unexpected when the phone rang, and I was seldom disappointed.

The relationship between Jimmy and me grew. Jimmy would tell me he liked my "guts," liked the fact that I didn't appear to be afraid of him, liked that I challenged him. But most of all, Jimmy was impressed that I was a reporter who wasn't afraid to go after the truth.

There was something about Jimmy that reminded me of my father. It was certainly not the corruption and violence tied to Hoffa—my father never would have been involved in that activity. I think it was the physical toughness of the man, a man then in his sixties and built like a stone wall. His hands were working man's hands—strong, vein-bulging hands symbolic of the blue collar middle class worker, of the old world hard work ethic.

It was a hell of a year, 1975. It began when I asked Jimmy to do an interview for *Playboy Magazine*. His initial reaction was classic Hoffa. "I don't want to be in a magazine with tits on the back of my picture."

I assured Jimmy that would not be the case and he agreed to do the interview. When it ran in December, 1975, it made *Playboy* history, selling over six million copies.

We sat in his newly-remodeled kitchen at his home in Lake Orion, Michigan. Jimmy was proud of the kitchen and talked about it as he made coffee for us.

After pouring coffee, Jimmy sat down.

"You ready?" I asked.

"Yeah."

"I've only got one condition," I said.

"Yeah? What's that?" He asked, his voice sounding tougher.

"That you answer every and all questions."

"No problem," he growled, "just remember—you gotta live with the answers."

Never for a minute, for a second, did I think it would be his last interview, that people would be reading Hoffa's thoughts and comments coming from the grave.

So candid, my reporting on Jimmy was examined for clues and became part of the file the FBI has on me. Both the mob and the authorities wondered what I knew about Hoffa and his enemies that didn't appear on the printed page. By no measure of the imagination did I ever think my life could get so wild, so crazy.

On July 30, 1975, Jimmy Hoffa mysteriously disappeared. There was talk of kidnapping, mob hits, grand juries, and graveyards. By October my obsession with Hoffa, the Teamsters and the mob was clear, just as clear as the word on the street that said Jimmy had given me information to use in case something happened to him, insurance so to speak. How that rumor began I don't know. What I did know was I found myself caught right smack at the collision point of union politics, mob dominance, and one of the most concerted law enforcement efforts in history.

Just as clear was that within weeks of his disappearance, I ended up facing four years in prison charged with a felony for carrying a gun. Yeah, I was obsessed all right, and had absolutely no idea of the nightmare of mystery and international intrigue that was about to come my way. Jimmy Hoffa sure put a spark in my life!

It was a week that seemed to last a year, the week of July 27, 1975. On Monday the 28th, my boss, Don Patrick, a fellow reporter, and I decided to "investigate" a few topless bars in town. We had been working hard and felt like a little rest and relaxation was in order.

As we drove down Cass Avenue in the heart of Detroit we were monitoring the police radio. Suddenly we heard a call for backup help at a bar on Livernois Avenue on the west side. The report said the initial call was a shooting in progress.

"Let's go!" I shouted at Patrick, who reacted by immediately hanging a hard right turn.

Ten minutes later we were a block from Bob Bolton's bar on Livernois and could see that a riot was quickly becoming reality.

It was a battleground. Police cars, fire engines, burning buildings and mobs of people. Patrick pulled the car right smack into the middle of the melee behind a fire engine. It was not the place to be. Bang! Thump! Something hit the car—once, twice, again. I opened the door and started to get out when a huge chunk of concrete came flying at me. I ducked and it slammed into the roof of the car.

"Let's get the hell out of here," I screamed. It was raining concrete bombs. Patrick threw the car in reverse and as we started backing up a black guy yelled at me.

"Help!"

"Come on," I yelled at the guy stranded in the street. He started running alongside the car. As we picked up speed, I reached out and grabbed his arm; struggling, I managed to pull him halfway into the car.

Patrick backed up a good half a block. We all bailed out with tape recorders rolling, recording for history what could have been the start of Part Two of the famous 1967 Detroit riots.

Fires now were spreading from building to building. People were throwing things, sirens were screaming; it was a war zone.

Bam, bam, bam—gunshots exploded as I ran across the street into a gas station. A car was burning in front of me, a police helicopter hovered overhead. Boom! Tear gas filled the air . . . boom, boom, more tear gas!

Pulling a handkerchief from my back pocket, I covered my mouth and nose, then leaned up against a gas pump to catch my breath. Police cars raced around the pumps with tires screeching. I felt like I was in a wagon train with Indians circling and attacking. It was surreal.

With all the fires burning, I suddenly realized I had picked a less than desirable spot to rest—between two gas pumps. I decided to make a run for it.

Dodging between two police cars, I ran to a phone booth about fifty yards from where I'd started. I called the ABC Radio news desk in New York and yelled, "roll tape."

As I was reporting the story to the network, someone set a car on fire about ten feet from the phone booth. The crowd outside the booth was getting uglier as they cheered the growing fire.

"A car has been set on fire," I shouted into the phone. "It's about ten feet from where I am standing."

The angry crowd started banging on the phone booth and screaming obscenities.

I continued my report, as the crowd tried to knock the phone booth and me over. On top of that, I feared the car burning next to me was about to explode.

I slammed the phone down, and more stupid than smart, forced the door open and pushed into the crowd. I was screaming.

"What the hell is wrong with you? I'm a reporter."

Not many of the fine folks were attentively listening. And I quickly realized that no one gave a shit about what I was saying.

I felt a blow across the back of my head. Falling to my knees, black, then white, spots filled my vision. I was kicked in the ribs and head a couple of times before I felt a hand grab the back of my shirt at the neck. Pulling me up to a standing position, a black guy was yelling.

"Back up, motherfuckers, back up. He's a good guy. Leave him be."

Somehow the man pulled me to the side of the street as the crowd lost interest in me and turned their attention back to the rioting.

Still stunned, I leaned against a building. My rescuer smiled at me and melted into the crowd.

Boom! More tear gas as more police arrived. There were now numerous fires burning.

"Hey, you all right?" Patrick yelled, coming up from my side.

"I think so but I got hit in the fuckin' head. Let's pull back a block."

As we moved back, the other reporter with us caught up. Looking around I saw madness, confusion and danger. We decided to stay on the perimeter until the police got things under control, which they did temporarily around one in the morning.

We later learned that the whole violent disturbance, which would continue off and on for days, began when the owner of Bob Bolton's bar shot a young black man. The bar owner said 18-year-old Obie Wynn was trying to break into the owner's car. Wynn died just before dawn.

Late morning, Thursday, July 31, 1975. I headed down to the Cass Corridor, one of the worst sections of Detroit. I was working on a documentary telling the story of hookers, pimps and drugs. The street was quiet and just after noon I called the office.

"It's quiet," Don Patrick said. "The only thing you got, Jerry, is a message to call 338-1776. The guy didn't leave a name but he sounded like a heavy."

"Got it, thanks," I said. "You know, I'm exhausted from that bullshit riot. I almost died in the street and I'm asking myself, for what? So a few thousand people can hear about violence and death on the street and say, 'Oh, that's too bad' and then go about their business? Forget it. There's gonna be some serious thought on my part before I jump into anything dangerous again."

"You're just tired," Don answered. "You can't say no to action, I don't care what you say."

"I mean it, Don, I really mean it." I hung up and dialed the number Don had given me.

"Yeah?" He sounded like a man who smoked three packs a day. His voice was more of a whiskey/cigarette voice than Patrick's and Patrick did smoke three packs a day. It was the voice of a man I knew, a good source who didn't bullshit.

"It's me. How ya doin?"

"Jerry, they got the little guy." The tone of his voice told me he was serious and very worried.

"Jesus, Jimmy Hoffa is dead?"

"I hope not, Jerry," the voice said. "He didn't come home last night. That's about all I know."

The day after Jimmy Hoffa disappeared, I bought a .38 caliber pistol, registered it with the police department and was told I needed a CCW, a concealed weapons permit. The cop then told me not to bother applying for a CCW because I wasn't a doctor carrying narcotics, or a businessman transporting large amounts of cash.

"What about being killed?" I asked, "does that count for anything to the CCW people?"

"Nope," he said, "that's why the police are around to protect."

I left the station. Opening the car door, I slid the gun under the driver's seat where it would stay.

The light changed from green to yellow just as I hit the intersection. Five seconds later a red light flashed on behind me. What the hell was going on? Detroit's finest don't make traffic arrests, I thought, pulling over.

Watching through the rearview mirror I saw two cops get out and walk up to the car, one on each side of it.

"License and registration please," the cop on my side of the car said.

"Why are you stopping me?" I asked, handing my license to him.

"You ran the red light."

"The light was yellow, not red."

"Where's your registration?"

"I guess it's in the glove box. WXYZ owns the car."

As the glove box opened the plastic bag of bullets fell out. It was a big hit.

"You got a gun in the car?" shouted the cop on the passenger side stepping back and reaching for his gun.

"Yeah, under the seat," I said. I was absolutely sure that after I explained the situation to the officers there would be no problem.

So much for being sure.

"Hands on the steering wheel and don't move," the cop on my side commanded loudly. "Move, get 'em up, now!"

These guys weren't kidding. The cop on the passenger side leaned into the car and reached under the driver's seat as his partner held his gun on me.

As the cop backed out of the car holding my .38, his partner said, "OK. Out of the car and move to the back."

I did.

"Against the trunk, feet spread eagle."

Then he frisked and handcuffed me. Jesus, this is too much, I thought, these guys are serious.

The 13th Precinct was the absolute worst jail in town. It was where the infamous Purple Gang had been locked up one night in the 1930's. Now, it was the unwilling gathering place for some of the hardest core, low life humans in Motown. Drunks, drug addicts, cutters, killers—and me.

I was fingerprinted and my mug shot taken. The jailer put me in a large cell with a couple of other prisoners. One man lying in the corner looked dead.

Standing in the center of the cell, I looked at the other inmate. He smelled like vomit, urine and stale beer. He had a big wet spot on his crotch area. This congenial fellow wanted to chat.

"Whatta they got ya' here for?" he mumbled drunkenly. God, he stunk.

"I had a gun in my car," I said.

"Ya had gum in yor car?" He looked bewildered, belched and slipped back down onto the floor. I just shook my head and walked to the other side of the cell.

Sitting there thinking, I started getting angry. The jailer came back into the room. "Why the hell was I arrested when someone was trying to kill me?" I screamed at the jailer.

"Shut the fuck up," he offered sympathetically and walked out.

"Don't I even get a tin cup so I can bang on the bars?" I shouted and was answered by the iron door slamming shut.

About 30 minutes later Mr. Warmth, the jailer, came back and took me to the detective bureau where I met a Sgt. Harris. In a half hour, Sgt. Harris had checked with Southfield, Michigan police, the town where I lived, and verified that personal protection was being provided for me and my family after we received threats.

"I'm going to release you," Harris said, "with a strong recommendation that you apply for a concealed weapons permit or else don't carry the gun."

"Thanks, I appreciate your understanding."

As I was starting to leave the station, a half a dozen cops wearing flack vests and carrying shotguns came running down the hall looking like they were headed for big time action.

"What's happening?" I asked a sergeant standing by the desk.

"Just a drug bust, no big deal," he answered.

"I wanna go with them."

"Jesus, you just were a fuckin' prisoner," the sergeant said. "Now you wanna go on a bust?"

He thought for a minute, shrugged his shoulders and said. "You got the press credentials, so why not. Maple, Gaide, take Stanecki with you."

I got into the back seat of the police cruiser. It felt familiar—it was the same police car I had been a prisoner in a couple of hours earlier.

The drug bust didn't turn out to be much except the police sure busted up an apartment. It made me angry watching cops pull and dump drawers, throw mattresses and knock chairs over. It also made me realize how miserable a cop's job was and how easy it would be to develop a "life's a shit sandwich" attitude.

I went home one tired cowboy that night thinking all was OK.

The next morning the phone rang. It was Sgt. Harris.

"There's a little problem here, Jerry. It seems someone dropped a dime on you and the newspapers are pushing on us hard. They're saying the chief got involved last night to kick you."

"That's not true," I said "I was released after police verified what I had said about police protection was true."

"I know, you know," Harris said, "but, apparently some asshole here called the newspaper. I was told to contact you and tell you to come back in 'cause this has to go downtown to the prosecutor's office."

"What?"

"I know, it's a pain in the ass but it's gotta be handled this way. I'm pretty sure nothing will happen at the prosecutor's except they'll talk to you and then not charge you."

I didn't like the sound of anything I was hearing. I didn't have money for an attorney and didn't think the station would pay for my defense on a CCW charge.

By three o'clock that afternoon things were progressively worse. I was standing in front of a judge charged with carrying a concealed weapon, a felony with mandatory prison time on conviction. I stood mute to the charge and was released on a $1,000 personal bond. I walked out of the Murphy Hall of Justice that day facing a two-year mandatory prison sentence with the possibility of two more years tacked on.

I went home shocked, thinking that I would be financially ruined because of legal fees, and that I would be railroaded into prison time.

✦ ✦ ✦

I was down, but then I found a friend I didn't know I had. Bob Pavich, a reporter for *The Detroit News*, offered to talk to Armand Bove', an attorney representing the police sergeants' union. Armand, along with his partner, Ralph Nelson, offered to help—pro bono.

That moment, that day, these guys became my only hope. I felt a little better.

For the next year the whole mess grew more and more into a mountain, adding more fuel to the flame of insanity and madness that made up my life.

Time and time again we went to court as rumors floated that outside influences were leaning on the court to nail me. One friend told me an FBI agent who "hated my guts" was trying to influence the case. And, that the FBI agent was getting help from a television reporter who was working for my sister station, WXYZ-TV.

Finally, after almost a year of legal battles and motions, on October 19, 1976, Judge Henry Heading stated from the bench that he was angry with outside forces who were trying to prejudice the case against me. With that statement, he dismissed the charges. There had been no just cause and my constitutional rights had been violated. No Miranda rights had been given.

As I think back, there were a lot of people who cared about me, cared enough to honor me with many awards. Unfortunately, I didn't care enough about me to really appreciate them—the people, the awards.

From Emmys to Humanitarian of the Year presented by Eastern Michigan University, along with dozens of other awards, never found a place on my walls or in a display case. I hid them all away in boxes because I felt then that I didn't deserve them. I'd always felt that I wasn't doing enough or helping enough people.

In those days, if you would have told me I had a self-esteem problem, I would have laughed and said you were crazy. Of course, if you said I had a drinking problem, I would *not* have laughed and said you were crazy. How could I have a drinking problem? I was a TV star. Research showed 70% of the people watching TV knew who I was, liked me, respected me.

Sadly, I didn't feel any of the love because of the intense internal pain and confusion I felt trying to be all, to all.

The emotional pain grew; I drank more and smoked marijuana trying to ease the pain and the confusion. Insanity? Naw, not to me, not then.

In the summer of 1979 we took a two week vacation. I'd finally gotten smart enough to realize I needed two weeks at a time to come down. It took the first seven days for me to unwind from the intensity of work.

This time, the two weeks didn't help. A migraine headache was relentless and I was taking the strongest prescribed pain killer available. For seven days the pain never took a break. It was so bad I couldn't drive a car.

Back at work, I was more exhausted than before. I vividly remember the day it all came tumbling down. Standing in the center of my office feeling absolute and total desperation, I knew I was in deep trouble.

I picked up the telephone and dialed the number of my oldest friend, John Manis, a doctor in San Francisco. John answered on the second ring.

"John," I struggled to talk, "I never thought I'd say this, but I need help."

I started sobbing as John listened helplessly 2,500 miles away.

"Hang on, Jerry," he said, "I'll call you back soon."

A short time later the phone rang. It was John. He'd made arrangements with a psychiatrist named Peter Walsh, who would be happy to help.

A week later I was "on vacation" again. I flew to San Francisco to do intensive therapy with Peter.

I had gone 2,500 miles to get help because I was afraid that if management at the television station knew I was in trouble they would look at me as damaged goods.

I was also worried that the newspaper gossip columns would be printing things that would be detrimental to me, my family and career.

I remember the first two days I was in California. I stayed with John and his wife, Frannie, as I usually did. This time there was no pleasure.

While waiting until Peter cleared his schedule and shuffled appointments so we could work for hours at a time, I drove north from San Francisco on the coastal highway. It's a magnificent drive with an incredible view of the Pacific Ocean. I hardly noticed it.

I stopped at a small motel in Gualala for the night and drank, trying to kill the pain, not realizing I was too numb to feel the alcohol. I drank a lot but couldn't get relief until I feel asleep. In reality, I had passed out from the booze.

By six the next morning I was walking in a cool fog on a desolate and deserted beach. I'd always loved the beach, loved the feeling of power and energy of the ocean. This morning however, all I felt was the wet from the mist and fog that covered the beach and my life. I was completely emotionally and physically numb.

For days I'd had no appetite. When I did eat, the food had no taste. I had no desire to live, but I wasn't thinking of killing myself.

My work with Peter—two, sometimes three hours at a time, brought some immediate relief as I started to understand a few things.

For five days we worked and did psychological testing. It was slow going because the depression was so deep. But we made progress. Then it was time to go home.

I made arrangements with Peter to continue weekly therapy sessions via the telephone and headed home.

As the 727 lifted out of the San Francisco fog that day, an incredible thing happened about twenty minutes into the flight. I look at it now as truly a deep spiritual experience.

I was emotionally drained and very fragile. I reached over and picked up the music headset, turning up the volume.

Melissa Manchester was just starting to sing a song I'd never heard. Looking down at the majestic snow-capped Sierra Nevada Mountains, the words from Melissa's journey embraced my soul:

*I wake up and see*
*The light of the day shining on me,*
*Make my own time—it's mine to spend.*

*Think to myself (my own best friend),*
*"It's not so bad all alone comin'*
*Home to myself again."*

I began to cry. Goose bumps appeared on my arms. Rubbing my arms, a feeling of being safe started moving through me.

*Now, I understand*
*whatever I feel is whoever I am.*
*Watching my life and how it's grown,*
*Lookin' on back to things I've known.*
*It's not so bad all alone comin'*
*Home to myself again.*

*It's not so bad to get lost in my tears,*
*And to laugh and to cry*
*For the years gone by.*
*Oh, my. Oh, my . . .*

Not wanting anyone to see me crying, I pressed my forehead tightly to the plane's window. Weeping softly, I listened to the words that seemed written just for me.

*Now, somehow I know*
*I've come a long way—got a long way to go,*
*But somethin' inside is makin' me strong,*
*And in the bad times, I'll get along,*
*'Cause it's not so bad all alone comin'*
*Home to myself*
*Again.*

*I'm comin' home.*

At that moment I knew I would survive. Thank you, Melissa. Thank you for bringing me hope.

✦ ✦ ✦

Praise for my work continued yet I felt more and more worthless. I just didn't believe people meant their kind and good words. For my work, maybe—but for me—no way.

I will never forget the last Emmy I won.

It was a Saturday in spring, 1981. I awoke restless, nervous. I was unaware at that time that my nervousness was really fear. Fear to me in those days was if someone stuck a gun in my face and cocked the hammer. That was fear. I had no idea that 99% of the time, when I was feeling out of sorts, nervous, anxious, restless, whatever, it was because of fear.

It was the third year in a row that I was nominated for an Emmy. I'd won the other years and something told me that I would win again. To this day I don't know why I knew, I just knew.

By noon the day of the Emmys, I decided to drink a little wine to relax. I drank a bottle of Chardonay.

By three o'clock I was really troubled so I smoked a joint to mellow out. There, that felt better . . . for a few minutes. Then I started getting paranoid. Oh boy, what am I going to do now? Thinking I'd found the solution, I took a Tranzene—a mild tranquilizer—to take the edge off. Yup, you guessed it. Everything got worse.

Carolyn, my wife, and I headed for the awards with me behind the wheel.

At the cocktail party before the awards I drank a couple of glasses of cheap white wine. That did it. It was the cheap white wine that made me do what I did.

Of course I'm being sarcastic.

By the time my category came around I was slouched down in the seat, my head spinning. I was filled with fear—panic actually, except I didn't know what the hell panic really was. I was just nervous, I thought. I glanced at my wife and saw a frozen, "God, I hope it's going to be all right" smile on her face.

"The winner is . . . Jerry Stanecki, The Newshawk, for his story on Autism." Applause, lots of it. Loud, scary applause.

I jumped up and jogged down the aisle, never thinking of walking, high energy—always my style.

To this day I really can't explain what happened next or what possessed me to do *it* or why I did *it*, and *it* was the closest to self annihilation any human could get. And I did *it* on stage.

I glanced down and noticed that the president of the National Academy was dozing in his seat. Maybe that's what triggered me to react, to shock; I don't know, but insanity took over.

"This is bullshit!" I said, holding up the highest award a reporter could win, "Instead of spending time giving ourselves awards, we need to be out there helping more people."

I had just dumped the maximum load on my peers, insulting those who had honored me with the recognition of excellence. I heard gasps. The audience was stunned. The president was awake, and I was headed off the stage and out the side door.

Leaving my wife sitting in the theater, I drove down to the Old Parthenon restaurant in Greektown, a three-block strip of restaurants in the heart of Detroit. One of the owners, Tommy Peristeris, was a good friend, and I needed to talk.

Too ashamed to go in the front door, I found myself behind the restaurant in a filthy, rat infested, garbage-littered alley soaking wet from the rain.

I pushed my way through the garbage in the alley and banged on the back door of the restaurant. Minutes went by, rain drops covered my tears. Part of me hoped Tommy wouldn't hear the knock and part of me prayed he would.

As Tommy opened the door, the light from inside the restaurant cast a spotlight on me. Soaked from the rain, my tuxedo drooped, my bow tie somewhere lost.

"Jesus, man, what happened to you?" Tommy's eyes were wide open, a look of alarm on his face.

"I fucked up big time," I said, sneaking into the restaurant.

Tommy listened in disbelief as I told him the story. When I finished, he didn't say a word.

"Jesus God, Tommy, what am I gonna do?"

He put his arms around me; hugging me he said, "Don't worry, it's gonna to be all right, it's gonna work out."

It was then I realized just what a good friend Tommy was. His arms around me brought a glimmer of hope to a beaten man in a hopeless situation. I cried, he comforted me.

Waking up Sunday I was filled with guilt, shame and fear. Deep in my gut I knew I had done a hell of a job of destroying myself and my career. Impending doom was roaring through me like a tidal wave.

What I didn't do in beating myself up, the newspapers did for me. The stories were truly damning and some just plain cruel. It hurt a lot.

Carolyn was filled with fear and sadness. She had to be ashamed of me for what I had done, yet was kind enough to leave me alone.

Sunday was a day of terrible remorse, shame and pure terror. I had 24 hours to suffer before I had to face the firing squad at Channel 7.

First thing Monday morning, I walked into the news director's office.

"What in the hell were you trying to achieve?" Bob White asked.

"I have no idea, Bob," I answered. "All I know is I screwed up big time and I'll have to suffer the consequences, so I'll pay the price. All I want to do now is put this behind me and move on."

He just shook his head.

I could have been fired because of the morality clause in my contract but I wasn't. I guess I was making too much money for the station.

I didn't realize it then, but know today, that my life had gone from the dark side—investigating political corruption—to the darker side with violence and the murder of Hoffa—to the darkest side of life as The Newshawk, watching everyday people trying to screw each other.

As I think back, the craziness in my life comes into focus. Viewers loved my work and would constantly tell me so. I never felt worthy of any of the praise. All the old pictures I was raised with, about perfectionism and impossible self demands all set my mind up to say, it's not good enough, it's never good enough. Through it all, I felt *I* just wasn't good enough for people to accept and like. Jerry was lost!

Another insanity was the tremendous fear I had of financial insecurity. In 1982 I was making over $100,000 a year, and always worried that it wouldn't be enough to get by on, that I'd wake up broke and homeless.

❖ ❖ ❖

Nineteen Hundred Eighty Three was a year in my life never to be forgotten.

It began with my mother dying on Super Bowl Sunday. I quit a job and lost a career. I bought a mountain in north Georgia, and ended the year with divorce.

It was typically Milwaukee cold that January in 1983 when we buried my mother. The week before I'd received a call that she'd had a heart attack and was in bad shape. I flew home and the day after I arrived Mom passed.

To this day, I am still filled with gratitude that God gave me those two days with her—for during those days, Mom and I embraced our lives together, made amends and loved each other warmly.

When she passed I was deeply touched by the look on her face. All of life's pain, carved so deeply in her face, was gone. Looking thirty years younger, she was smiling the peaceful smile of a carefree little girl.

At the funeral, as befits Catholic tradition, a holy card showing the person's date of birth and the date of death is given out.

I thumbed through about twenty samples, moving quickly, wanting to be done with it, when suddenly I stopped and knew instantly I'd found the card. It was a prayer Mom had often mentioned that she really liked and found deeply powerful.

Mom worried a lot about my drinking and asked me several times to slow down. I ignored her and was irritated with her "nagging" me.

I didn't realize what I'd done that day when I picked the holy card for Mom. I know today, without question, what my loving mother was still trying to tell me.

The card I selected, without a second thought, was *The Serenity Prayer*.

The former news director from WXYZ, Phil Nye, was now the station manager at KGO-TV, San Francisco, another station owned by the ABC Radio Network. The news director at KGO was Pete Jacobus, an old acquaintance of mine who liked my work. Pete was a man I thought of as a friend.

"You've got to come out here, Jerry." Pete said via long distance, "we need the Hawk here."

I had wanted to move to San Francisco for years and now I had a solid opportunity. I instructed my agent to see what he could do.

My agent and Nye, as news director in Detroit, had gone head to head on my previous contract. Nye made it clear that he disliked my agent, but the deal was done. Later, I learned that Nye had felt humiliated by the Detroit deal. "Later" was after the San Francisco surprise came.

As a condition for me to get the San Francisco job, since both stations were owned by ABC, I had to agree to not negotiate the Detroit station against the San Francisco station.

Detroit was offering $105,000 for the first year, with healthy annual increases for the next two years. Very good money for a non-anchor in 1983.

I called Jacobus and told him the amount of money that was on the table in Detroit.

"Don't worry about the money," Pete said, "that's no problem, we'll match it."

I agreed to drop negotiations with WXYZ and accepted the San Francisco job.

The next day my agent called me with the surprise "Nye just called and said, 'send him out, we'll pay him $80,000 a year.'"

Nye had his revenge against my agent . . . I paid the price.

I had been betrayed, but was so exhausted I couldn't find the energy to fight back—to get even.

I was tired, very tired, but would never admit that I was burned out from six years of being The Newshawk. Six years, with an emotional crash in 1979, and still I believed I could handle anything. Hell, I was superman, wasn't I?

I walked out of WXYZ in the spring of '83 full of emotional pain—angry, betrayed, abandoned. On top of it, I couldn't go a day without taking a drink, all in an effort to ease the pain.

I decided that I would take it easy for awhile. I told myself I would plant flowers, and wake up each day when I wanted. Life would be eating fresh fruit in the morning and drinking a little wine at night. The good life—I deserved it.

I bought a mountain instead.

Yup, 350 acres of beautiful mountain on the Alabama-Georgia border near Rome, Georgia. Indian Mountain had three natural springs on it and one road into it.

I planned to put a house trailer near the top of Indian Mountain, barricade the road and sit there, in the middle of the woods on the mountain, build a house and write. I was going to simplify my life.

Looking back, I didn't have a very good start at the simple life. I didn't buy the trailer in Georgia, that would have been too easy. I bought it in Detroit so that I would have to haul it 750 miles.

Jerry Don Dempsey, my wife's cousin, drove to Detroit in his pickup to help.

Jerry Don is a mountain man. I think he finished the third grade before he quit school. He can't read or write but he can tell you if an animal track was made by a gray or red fox.

He is a stubborn, independent man who never let lack of education stand in his way. For example, when he got angry at the Alabama power company because the bill was too high, Jerry Don and his wife Peggy Sue built a water wheel and mill from scratch and made their own power.

A week after we got the trailer to Georgia, before we could move it to the mountain, another crisis came. There was a clash of wills between my wife and me. We'd been trying to work the troubles out of our marriage for five years, but it wasn't happening.

That scene, that morning in the Georgia heat, was the final scene between Carolyn and me. That day, my marriage ended after nineteen years.

Let's see, no job, no income, no mountain escape, no marriage. What next?

It came in the form of a phone call from Jeanne Findlater, the Vice President General Manager of WXYZ-TV.

Jeanne was the first woman to run a major market television station. A wonderful woman, she was a strong supporter of commitment to community and locally produced television. She was a friend and believed in my work and me.

"Are you done screwing around?" Jeanne asked. "You have to come back to work."

Jeanne told me the people needed me, needed what I brought to them. She said I could do whatever I wanted to, just as long as I got back on the air.

I went back to work for WXYZ-TV and from 1984 through 1987, told stories of courage, of struggle, of people fighting the odds and winning. All the time I was drinking . . . held hostage by denial.

Since those denial days in '87, I've learned that one of the last things a person trapped in alcoholism gives up or loses is the job. As long as the person continues to work, the denial of "I don't have a problem with booze" is fed.

Life went on and I grew more miserable and didn't know why.

The changes began when my life finally got too insane. It was when I was fired.

At the same time, a three year love affair I was involved in fell apart. Out of work, out of love, depressed and scared, I was down and the count was eight.

That's when my friend Brannon came to visit.

It was August 28, 1987, the day I finally broke through the denial and admitted I couldn't handle drinking anymore. I remember it like it was yesterday.

"Why don't you call Dennis Wholey," Brannon suggested. "He's been in television and dealt with his alcoholism and TV."

Dennis had written *The Courage To Change*, a book of celebrities' stories and their battles with alcoholism. The book was a smash and on the *New York Times Bestseller List* for months.

"Naw," I said. "We had a disagreement about ten years ago when we were both working for Channel 7. He doesn't want to hear from me."

Although we had talked a couple of times during the years, I felt Dennis didn't like me.

What Brannon said next made me decide to call Dennis.

"I'm sure Dennis would be delighted to hear from you."

Wow, I thought, delighted to hear from me—I didn't believe that—but for some reason, I just had to test what Brannon said.

I called Dennis and the call showed me I had, again, been thinking the wrong way.

After "hello's, how are you's?" Dennis asked what he could do for me.

"I've got a situation. I'd like to look at it," I said. I couldn't even say, "I've got a drinking problem." No denial there, huh?

"What's that?" he asked.

I blurted it out.

"I can't stop drinking," I said, not knowing what he would say. Dennis didn't miss a beat.

"I've been waiting for you," he replied.

We laughed and talked awhile about life and recovery. He was comforting, encouraging. Dennis then asked if I could "hold off" until the following Tuesday. I said sure, and he asked if he could take me to a meeting where a few men—recovering from alcoholism—sat and talked.

The following Tuesday it was raining hard. Dennis picked me up and drove me to an old mansion in one of the worst sections in the heart of the city.

Walking into the mansion, irony struck as I remembered sitting in front of a fire in the same parlor years before. It was here I had done a TV story on Father Vaughn Quinn, who ran the treatment center the building housed.

A dozen men sat around a table that Tuesday. They welcomed me warmly and told me I was the most important person there. I didn't really understand what they meant, but felt OK with it.

What happened next amazed me. As each man spoke in turn, he talked about how *I* was feeling—each man, incredibly, was telling my story.

Hmm, I thought, how considerate. Dennis must have called the men over the weekend and told them my story so they'd say things to make me feel comfortable. When I realized that was absolutely not the case—that each man was talking about himself and his life—I knew that I was in the right place.

I had taken the first step toward recovery; I had admitted I was powerless over alcohol *and* I had asked for help. I felt like ten zillion pounds had been lifted from my back. I was ready to begin traveling the amazing, exciting road of recovery.

On that night, August 28, 1987, when a beaten man, filled with total desperation and hopelessness, angry that he could not go one day without a drink, honestly surrendered—a remarkable thing happened.

The desperate, constant craving that demanded I drink . . . completely disappeared.

What happened to me—was a miracle.

∾

# Today

*What you've just read is some of my yesterday. The following pages of this book pretty much explain how I live my life today.*

It occurs to me that someone reading this might think that writing what I have was a show of bravado and how fearless I've been in my life. Don't make that mistake.

What I've tried to do is give you highlights of the insanity a person caught in the throes of addiction goes through. I hope it gives you a feel for the madness that led me to the credentials for what I speak and write about.

The journey to sobriety and serenity wasn't an easy one. It's been painful, happy and sad. But then, if the journey had been easy, I probably would have gotten bored and quit.

It's been a journey one-day-at-a-time. One filled with hundreds of support group meetings. With willingness to learn a new way of thinking, developing trust and a lot of faith, I've exposed my secrets and made myself vulnerable to strangers who, I discovered, were far from that.

These "strangers" accepted me unconditionally, accepted me for who I was, and loved me until I learned how to love myself.

Some of the lessons learned are shared in the following pages— new ways of thinking, of living. I suggest you take your time reading this book. Jump around from story to story if you'd like, because there's no worry about finding out "the butler did it."

The life stories and thoughts are for you to enjoy and use. Let each story work for you. Feel the feelings they provoke, see how each applies to you, and use what you discover for your benefit.

If you find yourself getting uncomfortable about your life—good. Be gentle with yourself and patient. What you are supposed to learn will come if you are willing and available to it.

Remember . . . how you live your life is your choice. I feel strongly that a happy, joyous and free life is all about progress, not perfection.

For me,
it's *not* the final destination.

I don't want
to lay on my death bed
and finally feel happy.

I want the happiness today
and each day.

The secret to life
is to enjoy
the journey.

Dear Friends,

    I've included a few blank pages like this one throughout the book. Please use them for your thoughts.

# Understand Fear and Beat It

*Years ago, while on the Mississippi Bayou trying to catch alligator gar for a television news story, sound technician Jim Meredith asked if I was ever afraid of anything. "Not a thing," I said without a second thought. I was wrong.*

In those days of not understanding how subtle, cunning and powerful fear can be, I would just get upset or be a little anxious or "nervous," but never afraid. The real fears, the kind that ruin a day, an hour, even just a few minutes, were beyond my understanding.

Today, when something is troubling me, when I'm not feeling peaceful, it's because fear has me thinking I am not going to get what I want.

Ask yourself, are you peaceful, relaxed, feeling safe? If not, why not? What are you afraid of?

When I finally identified my simple fears—"gonna' be fired," "It's not going to be good enough," "What if," "I can't,"—then I could take action to eliminate the fear. How? I'd tell someone about my fears.

Tell someone? Sure. Just be sure that if you do unload your problems, it's someone you trust. I mean, if your boss comes up to you tomorrow and asks, "How are you doing, Joe?"

"Oh, I'm afraid," you answer honestly.

I suspect you might not get the desired response unless the boss is a friend.

Find someone with his or her act together enough to listen, acknowledge your feelings, and validate you for sharing your fears and your reality at that moment. Don't choose someone who will say, "Ah, you're really not afraid," or tell you, "That's crazy, you shouldn't feel like that." When you're feeling afraid you sure don't want someone to tell you you're not afraid, or that you are wrong for feeling the way you feel.

Often, too many of us have allowed others to tell us how we should feel. Conversely, many of us have been guilty of telling others how they should feel.

You want someone to support your true feelings, to remind you that it's OK to have them.

Amazing results can be had when you're feeling fearful and someone says, "I can understand how you might be feeling that way."

On the other side, if you tell someone and your trust is thrown back at you, try not to take it personally. At times, when we're feeling ultra-sensitive, if we don't consciously watch it, we allow others to trigger old pictures, old wounds that say—something is wrong with me.

For a lot of years, I—superman, machoman, "don't need nobody" man—helped a lot of people while always neglecting myself. I didn't need help from anyone; besides, I felt no one wanted to help me anyway. Fear.

It takes a strong person to trust enough to share fear. You could even say it takes a—fearless person.

છ

# Anxiety Fear and Faith

*While driving the other day my attention shifted to the radio. "Today is National Anxiety Day," the voice said and proceeded to interview a psychologist about anxiety. The psychologist talked about everything from panic to pumpernickel but never once mentioned the main cause of all anxiety.*

Fear wasn't mentioned once. It was very interesting.

When we are feeling safe and secure, we're not worried about money, children, job or life itself. We basically have no anxiety. However, for a lot of people these days that's about six seconds a day. If just one of those concerns or worries kicks in, then look out, here comes Mr. Anxiety.

The answer to anxiety is faith, honest-to-God full surrender faith, in a power greater than you. It's having faith that no matter how bad things are at that moment, it will work out.

One day, while playing in a celebrity golf tournament, Tim Allen came into the locker room complaining about how "they" wanted him to do a pilot of a "damn" sit-com (TV comedy show).

Tim didn't like the idea because he thought it would take away from his work on the road as a stand-up comic. He was sure that his stand-up work was the ticket to fame and fortune.

Anyway, against his will, he went ahead and shot the situation comedy pilot. You know what? Tim was right. The pilot did take away from his time on the road as a stand-up comic. That pilot became a weekly television show. A No. 1 smash hit show called "Home Improvement."

Sometimes it's hard to have faith when there is fear, especially when we think we know what's better for us.

∞

**F** alse
**E** vidence
**A** ppearing
**R** eal

# The Story of "Toilet Paper Tommy"

*"I've never told this to anyone before," Gino the Razor said in a conspiratorial tone. "But there was this kid in the neighborhood named Tommy. It was over on the east side where I grew up." A dozen men around the table leaned in and listened.*

George, also known as Gino the Razor, always told a good story. Some were hard to believe, others outrageous, always though, Gino's stories were entertaining.

"We called this kid 'Toilet Paper Tommy.'" Gino said, "because he always carried a little roll of toilet paper in his right front pocket.

"You see, what happened one day was that Tommy shit in his pants and his father, a drunk, beat him so bad—scared him so bad—that from that day on Tommy always carried part of a roll in his pocket."

A couple of the guys smiled nervous smiles, but most looked serious as they thought about what George was saying and their own issues. Especially their own "father" issues.

"Anyway, about three months ago I was on the east side for this and that, you know, and I spotted Tommy," George continued with his story. "He looked at me and said, 'George, how are you?'

"I looked at him, 'Tommy?'

"'To you, George,' Tommy replied, 'it's Toilet Paper Tommy.'"

George said they laughed, and he asked Tommy if he still had the toilet paper with him. "I mean, it's thirty years later, right?"

"'No,' said Tommy, explaining that his father had died. 'I don't have to carry that around anymore.' Tommy smiled."

This story reminded me of the fear I had as a boy. Fear that I would never get what I needed from my father; that I would never

hear quiet words of wisdom and guidance on how to handle becoming a man.

My fear proved to be correct as my father was absent or sick in
my early teen years and my mother, God bless her soul, there too
much.

To dwell on this or blame my father for not being there for me is
a complete waste of time and energy. Now is now and, like
Tommy, I don't need to carry "that" around anymore.

# Even the Worst of Times Can Be the Best of Times

*When you choose to believe that everything that happens to you is happening for your good, life becomes much easier.*

"Today was a day of terror," Julie said. "I was filled with panic."

Julie was talking about her struggle with addiction. She had gone two months without giving in, but the night before had been a real challenge to her sobriety.

"When I get this way, I get crazy." Julie explained. "I don't know what I want, I don't know where I am going, I don't know where I am, I don't know who I am, or what I am." She was spinning with confusion, fear and panic.

"Give yourself credit for not making the turn into the 7-11 convenience store to buy booze," I said, and told her the story of my friend, Vinnie, and his adventure with a bad hamburger at a classy country club.

Vinnie made his stomach-churning discovery that the burger he'd eaten fifteen minutes before was bad as he and an important client approached the first green.

"It was terrible," Vinnie recalled. "I was totally overcome by urges to go and I panicked. I drove the golf cart across a green, for God's sake, to get to the men's room faster."

Suffering, Vinnie was struggling, using every ounce of energy to resist the effects of the food poisoning. He didn't like not having control of his body.

"I was sick as a dog," Vinnie said. "I was sitting on the john and at the same time upchucking in the wastebasket. I thought I was gonna die, I mean die."

The violent reaction to the food poisoning went on for thirty-five minutes before Vinnie could catch his breath.

It was like being in the eye of a hurricane.

"Suddenly, I decided I would try to enjoy what was happening, accept it as part of the journey, something I didn't like, but as something that was good for me."

Vinnie was getting more animated.

"I mean, my body was getting rid of what poisoned me and I couldn't, even if I wanted to, stop it. When I realized that, I felt grateful. Can you believe it? Grateful that I was so sick. Then I just relaxed and it all changed; it all got easier."

He had made a choice and taken action. Vinnie stopped resisting and surrendered. When he did, he relaxed. He had taken a terrible situation and made it easier when he stopped resisting.

Funny, so many times I think of Vinnie and his amazing discovery. Trust—stop resisting and enjoy the journey—the good with the bad.

You betcha, Vinnie. Thanks, pal.

"But what about the panic I experienced last night?" Julie asked.

"Have faith," I said, "faith that whatever is happening to you, as you process through the addiction, is all for your good. The panic, the pain, the fear. When you choose to be grateful for these experiences then the fear that causes the panic eases."

"Thanks." Julie said and smiled.

As we grow, make discoveries and find answers through surrender, just like Vinnie, we discover that it all gets easier when we stop resisting and accept what is.

When you choose to believe that everything happening is happening for your good, then it becomes good for you.

☙

# FEAR—Don't Let It Steal Your Happiness

*I got to thinking about it when I looked at the daily three-digit lottery number.*

Damn, look at that! The number for the evening drawing was 996. In my hand I was holding 969. I had played it both straight and boxed, which means I would have won—if only I—wait a minute. The fact is, I didn't.

What I did was go against my gut feeling to play the three numbers in the evening. Instead, I played the numbers at midday.

Close only counts in horse shoes, hand grenades and farts.

Oh well, back to reading the newspaper, I realized I was feeling funky. I was still irritated that I'd gone against my gut feeling on 969. Poor Me.

Forget it, it's no big deal. But I didn't forget it; I didn't allow myself to ignore what was making me uncomfortable.

I put the paper down. Why was I upset? Why was I belittling myself?

Let's see, I am disappointed. I mean I didn't get what I wanted. *But* I need the money, I rationalized. Aha! There it is—that old fear. *But* taxes are due, bills to pay, no steady income, etc.

Fear was stealing my happiness.

The fear I was experiencing had nothing to do with the moment. And that moment was the reality of my existence; that moment was my life. Yet, I was in yesterday with my regrets—if only I'd gone with my gut. And I was in tomorrow with my rationalizations—I need the money.

I sat down and started to write.

Thank you, God, for all you've given me in this moment. The reality of a beautiful home—warm on a rainy, cool spring morning.

I'm feeling good. I have health, a family that is safe for now, two cats, a car, and enough money to feel secure for today.

Poor me? No sir, lucky me, grateful me—I was feeling positive, safe, unafraid.

For a lot of years, I was afraid I wouldn't have enough money, and in thinking about it, it was always that I would not have enough money—tomorrow.

It's a fear, I think, that's very real for a lot of people. Work hard, save money, don't dare lose your job, don't overspend, because it will all help you get more so you can retire.

Boy, that's a lot of fear. The kind of fear that causes big time stress. Stress . . . that after a couple of months in retirement "Old Joe" suddenly clutches his chest and bites the dirt with *the big one.*

Or Judy, so excited that her retirement is just three weeks away—all those years of hard work and sacrifice—soon she can enjoy life. Except two and a half weeks before her retirement, Judy finds herself standing eyeball to eyeball with St. Peter.

Tomorrow steals my today. Yesterdays steal my today, and today, this moment, right now, is all I have, it is my life.

When I choose to think differently, when I choose to be free, instead of a prisoner of fear and self pity, I'm good, real good. No, I'm better than good, I'm feeling: great-full.

ల

# When Fear Knocks, Faith Must Answer

*Fear imprisons; faith liberates. Fear paralyzes; faith empowers. Fear disheartens; faith encourages. Fear sickens; faith heals.*

Putting down the meditation book and thinking about Harry Emerson Fosdick's words, I wondered if he was the "Fearless Fosdick" I remembered as a kid. Then I laughed.

Fearless Fosdick was a character in the Lil' Abner comic strip. Fosdick was a Dick Tracy look-alike who always had bullet holes in his hat. I related to that.

"One of the easiest ways to develop an alternative to fear is to ask ourselves during a moment of fear: 'What is the worst thing that could happen?'"

"How about dying?" I asked out loud to no one. That's what could easily happen.

The meditation was for June 5. That day, three years before, the good doctor told me I had "some blockage" in the arteries that led to my heart. She suggested I seriously consider surgery.

Ironic, I thought, reading the meditation, then realized it wasn't irony at all.

I had come to believe that things like this happen when there is a need. I had a need and was paying attention.

"What do I fear and why do I fear it? I know I am OK because I have identified my fear," it said.

Huh? No, no, I'm not OK. I'm afraid *because* I had identified my fear. They wanted to rip my chest open and cut on my heart and that scared the hell out of me, which is something Sister Mary Arnold from my school days would say is a good thing.

The "some" blockage turned out to be 100 percent on the right side and 70-90 percent blockage of the rest of the arteries. I'd had a heart attack and didn't know it. Another attack, the surgeon I'd been referred to said, and I'd be dead meat. Well, he didn't exactly use those words.

When fear knocks—faith must answer, came to mind as I remembered another experience years before. It had been the first time I'd put real, honest-to-God faith and trust in a power greater than me.

It was in 1987, and I had broken my neck.

How? Well—it was from not acting my age on a trampoline.

I had put off the surgery to fix my neck. Finally, the pain got so bad I was forced to take action. Again, I was in a precarious situation. One slip of the surgeon's hand and I could be paralyzed for life. I was scared.

I remember putting on the open-back hospital gown before neck surgery. After looking around to be sure no one was in the dressing room, I got down on my knees.

"Well, God, this is it. I have two choices. Either I stay scared, which probably is not good for healing, or I have faith in you." I can still feel the hardness of that cold tile floor on my bare knees as I told the boss, "I have faith, Lord."

Amazingly, I felt calm. The fear left long enough for the anesthesia to do its job. The surgery was successful and my neck is fine.

So, three years after the open heart surgery, I read again the meditation of June 5, the date I was faced with life or death. I smiled and turned the page back to the day before, June 4, and read what I had written in the meditation book two years after the surgery, "'98. Dr. called and said stress test excellent. Heart great—better than a 40-year-old."

Yup, I thought, if Harry Emerson Fosdick practices what he preaches then he really is old Fearless Fosdick.

Can you remember
the last time
you were afraid
while you were
laughing?

THINK DIFFERENTLY
THINK DIFFERENTLY
THINK DIFFERENTLY
THINK DIFFERENTLY
THINK DIFFERENTLY
THINK DIFFERENTLY
THINK DIFFERENTLY
THINK DIFFERENTLY
THINK DIFFERENTLY
THINK DIFFERENTLY
THINK DIFFERENTLY
THINK DIFFERENTLY
THINK DIFFERENTLY
THINK DIFFERENTLY
THINK DIFFERENTLY

# Angry at God

*"I'm not happy with my recovery," Al said to a group of men who sit together and talk life every Wednesday afternoon in a church hall.*

With that one statement, Al put enough negative energy into the room for us to realize that he was not in a good place.

"I've been clean for over two years and I shouldn't have to feel the way I do, or go through the shit I'm going through," Al complained.

"In a nutshell, I want what I want and I'm sick of having to work for it. I shouldn't feel this bad. I'm tired of working the [recovery] program."

Al told us about how, in an effort to not use drugs, he recently went to the Salvation Army Church to help with some remodeling. He was sent to a bathroom and told to remove the ceiling panels from the suspended ceiling. It was a big bathroom, he explained, with several four-foot fluorescent lights supported by the drop ceiling.

"As I'm removing the panels, I start thinking about Forest Gump, you know the scene where the guy with no legs is on the shrimp boat. He's up on the mast during a hurricane screaming, 'You call this a storm, God?'"

Al said he started mumbling out loud while working on the ceiling, "You call this pain, God? Can't you do better than this?"

Al was obsessing, saying over and over, "You call this pain, God, you call this pain?"

Al climbed on a chair and reached to take down a ceiling panel, all the time mumbling.

Suddenly the whole ceiling came crashing down. One of the big lights broke loose and swung down like a pendulum, smashing into Al's face, knocking him from the chair to the floor.

Lying there, covered with dirt and ceiling pieces, his face bleeding, Al looked up and yelled.

"THAT'S IT, GOD? You call that a hit? Can't you do any better than that, God?"

Al started laughing and we joined in; he was laughing at himself for being such a jackass, for being such a spoiled brat.

"I want what I want when I want it! Now, that's funny," Al said. "And then I thought about the last time I felt like this. It was well over a year ago, I got mad at God and called him all kinds of names and blamed him for all my problems.

"The day after pitching that fit, I ended up stoned," Al said.

The room was very quiet.

"I don't ever want to go back to that pain," Al said intensely, "I'm glad I can laugh at myself today."

∽

**There
is
nothing
positive
in
resentment**

# First Buck John's Resentment List

*I never really heard of resentment until I was 40 years old or so. The word just never came up in my life. What's that? What did I do when someone did something to hurt me? I got even.*

First Buck John, who got his nickname because he still has the first dollar he earned, was telling me about how he used to have an "enemies list."

"Hell, I figured if [former President] Nixon could have one, I could," John said. "I even wrote away to a publishing company that specialized in revenge."

Geez, I thought, listening to John, I'd never put that much effort into the scheme of things because I never let anyone get the best of me . . . or so I used to think.

Today, I clearly understand resentment and the huge negative effect it has on my life.

It simply gives others power over me.

Resentment is re-feeling old experiences that have registered in my perception . . . something someone did to hurt me.

Today, I no longer have time to allow others who hurt me to live in my life rent free.

ℰℐ

# Resentments Die Hard

*"My father was with no question the allied supreme commander," Larry said, a furrow developing on his brow. "He was the kind of guy who would say, when people are down, give them a kick in the side, it'll give them a reason to get up."*

Larry and I were talking about feelings, courage and the problem of not being able to say how you feel unless you have a couple of drinks.

Larry explained that he could really relate to "bottle courage" and how that came into play for him. The image of his family, he explained, wasn't exactly like something you'd see on Disney.

"My father was in the hospital and he was dying," Larry said softly. "He was lying in a bed surrounded by signs all over the place that said oxygen, no smoking. I looked at him and knew he was on his last breath. I mean, he had cancer and still smoked cigars."

I shifted in my chair to get more comfortable.

"That's when I remembered," Larry continued, "that when I wanted to smoke a cigar I had to leave the house. I had to stand on the porch like a goddamn sixteen-year-old behind the barn—and I was fifty years old." Larry's words rang hard with anger.

"He never, never acknowledged me for who I am. You know it's 'I buy you books, send you to the best schools and you're still stupid.'"

Larry got up, took a couple of steps, turned around and sat down.

"I looked at my father and suddenly his chest heaved and he turned all gray. His head went back and his eyes rolled, and I knew he was gonna go."

Larry was really worked up now. It was like he was back in that day, in that hospital room.

"I don't know why," Larry continued, a gleam coming into his eye, "but I pulled out a big cigar, walked over, leaned real close, poked him in the chest and said. 'Now, is it OK if I smoke?'"

Larry was defiantly grinning now, as I imagined he had been that day.

"His eyes rolled and his chest heaved as he came off the pillow like a goddamn Doberman," Larry paused. "Believe it or not, the bastard lived another three days. God, he was a prick."

Sometimes resentments die hard.

✺

# Rage in the Driver's Seat—Bullets in Church

*There are too many of us out there—people who have stuffed their anger for years until it has become rage—rage that causes friends and neighbors to do "out-rage-ous" things. It's scary out there.*

I was driving to the barber shop, doing about 30-35 m.p.h. on the freeway access road, when suddenly a white car shot off the freeway and cut across two lanes of traffic heading for my lane, the closest to the curb.

The white car cut off the vehicle on my left and didn't quite make it to the lane I was in.

In a heartbeat, the woman driving the white missile—behind me now—gave me the finger and starting mouthing what I assumed were obscenities. At the red light, I looked in the rearview mirror. She was still motioning at me. I got out and walked back.

"Is that necessary?" I asked.

"There was a fuckin' yield sign, you fucker," she screamed.

She went insane. What came out of this young madwoman's mouth you wouldn't put in a sewer.

I was stunned, and I'm no altar boy. All the time she was screaming, violently jabbing her finger at me.

I shook my head and said, "It must be sad having to live in you."

"Fuck you." She was shaking with rage.

Driving away, I wondered if the young woman had children? I cringed at the thought that she did. Hatred is not inherited, it's taught.

Peter the barber and Sharon the manicurist listened to the story.

"Everybody is full of rage." Sharon offered without a second thought.

"That may be, but we as a society are out of control," I said.

"You got that right," she answered.

Fred, the shoeshine man, sat in a spare barber's chair reading the sports page. Fred King is a man who doesn't get excited; he's about as laid back and gentle as any human can be.

"Fred, have you ever been angry enough to kill someone or even hurt someone?" I asked.

"What was that?" Fred King looked up.

He has a hearing problem from his Army days—Korean war—artillery.

I asked again.

"One time," Fred said.

We waited for him to continue; a good twenty seconds passed.

"When a crazed gunman shot and killed my wife."

Stunned, not Sharon, not Peter, nor I said a word.

"In church . . . 1982," Fred said calmly. "He killed my wife, Sammie. That's what I called her . . . been married more than thirty years and had five children. He shot and killed two other people, too, then shot and crippled my son for life."

Fred talked of the memory without anger, without resentment.

"He was a big man, maybe 6'7", all muscle. The preacher was talking to him 'bout jumpin' on the woman he was living with. When the preacher finished this man said, 'you had your say, now I'm gonna' have mine, loud and clear.' I still hear them words. He pulled out two guns and started shooting."

We waited for Fred to say more. He didn't.

I asked if he'd forgiven the killer and Fred thought for a few seconds. Then, slowly nodding his head, said yes.

"How?"

"I just did. I read it in the Bible," he said, smiling.

"Did you feel actual physical relief when you did?" I asked.

"Yes . . . yes I did."

Freedom in forgiveness. Forgiveness relieved Fred of self, of the very heavy pain of anger and revenge.

To reach forgiveness, I've been taught, one must accept the anger and try and understand what caused it. A lot of anger comes because you're not getting your way. Once you understand the anger, then you can choose to release it, instead of stuffing it. The key to releasing anger is to do so in a way that doesn't hurt someone else.

So, when the anger screams inside, act to understand . . . instead of reacting. Take a second and think—I'm going to act, not react and I'm going to treat that person like I would like to be treated, and that's not with anger.

Isn't there some kind of saying or motto that goes "do unto others . . ."

❧

# Criticism Hurts!

*What we say and what we don't say—whether we believe it or not—can have a very deep effect on people.*

Make it praise today, not criticism.

Praise and encouragement can help someone soar.

Criticism, even in jest, can be the final gust of wind that blows out the last flame of hope.

We are here to help, not discourage, each other.

&#8766;

# Naw, I Love You—A Lesson for Gino the Razor

*George, better known as Gino the Razor, is talking: "I remember when I was fifteen. I decided to take on my old man."*

I guess with a nickname like "Gino the Razor," it's not hard to imagine the unhealthy, dysfunctional background George came from.

"I said, 'All right old man,'" Gino said, eyebrow arching, "'it's me and you, head to head, motherfucker. I've had it and now I'm gonna kick your ass.'"

"Naw," the old man said, smiling at his son. "I love you son, I'm not going to do that, I'm not gonna fight you."

"I turned around and started walking away," Gino said, "and he hit me on the back of the head with a blackjack."

That was George's lesson in trust.

I have come to believe that *old pictures,* like this one George experienced, must be changed if life is to be better.

Where we come from, what we are taught, is the way we believe, the way we act, until we realize a need for change. When we accept a need for change and are willing to take action to make the change, then we are available to positive new pictures.

Are there old pictures in your life that need to be developed into healthy new pictures?

ço

# That Look

*Kim was telling me how she had been at a business meeting the night before and had met a lot of very nice older women.*

"That was a very good experience for me," Kim explained, "because of my past and the difficulty I've had with women doing things like giving me a disapproving look."

"That look," I said, "boy, I know exactly what you mean. That look really used to get to me. The difference for me now is when I get 'that look' I feel sorry for the person because I know they must be having gas pains."

Kim laughed.

"In the past," I continued, "'that look' meant that person was disapproving of me; today I know that person is feeling panic because he or she is trying to discreetly let the burp silently escape."

☙

# Fenkell Street Harry—It's the Little Things

*I sense a real need in people today to become more aware of how we might be cheating ourselves. One of the first steps is to recognize self-criticism. Another way is to understand how the little things affect us.*

Pepsi Dick sat at the end of the long table with a 16 oz. bottle of Pepsi in front of him, another bottle next to it, this one in a brown paper bag. Before the hour was up, Dick would drink both bottles, hence the nickname.

Dick was listening to a fella complaining about feeling jittery, anxious, jumpy. When he finished, Pepsi Dick offered this for thought.

"There was a fella in the program (a 12-Step recovery program) named Fenkell Street Harry," Dick explained. "Harry would get up every day, get dressed, walk down Fenkell Street to the bus stop, buy a newspaper, ride the bus to a meeting, then go on to work. He did this for sixteen years.

"One morning Harry woke up ten minutes late. He started feeling anxious and was upset that he overslept, so he started rushing around to make up time. He threw his clothes on and while tying his shoe, his shoestring broke. Now he was angry. He recognized the feeling of 'why me?' but was too hurried to give it much thought.

"He ran out the door just knowing that he was going to miss his bus. When he got to the bus stop his friend Joe was standing there. The bus was late.

"By now Harry was thoroughly upset, angry, and frustrated. His ego roared into action. He had rushed and fussed, got upset and now the damn bus was late. Harry resented that.

"Harry bought his newspaper just as the bus pulled up. Sitting, he started to calm down, knowing his meeting was just a few minutes away. He opened his newspaper and stared in shock. It was yesterday's newspaper. That's when Harry lost it.

"The very next stop, Harry got off the bus, went into a bar, and never came back. He died not too long after, drunk.

"It's not the big issues in life that cause us problems," Dick said, smiling and slowly taking a drink of his Pepsi, "It's the little things."

℘

# Good Morning, World

*And then there are the other "little things" that make the difference.*

Walking out the front door one morning a few minutes after five, I was instantly struck by the force. It was absolute, complete and total silence. So quiet it was actually deafening. It was incredible.

Never before—ever—had I experienced silence like that. It reminded me of a scene from a science fiction movie. It was eerie.

There was nothing. No distant hum of traffic, no birds, no wind, nothing. It was magnificent and a little scary.

This is the city, for God's sake, I thought. There has to be noise. Any noise. Some noise. There was none.

I'd been in the desert—hundreds of miles from any town, any human—and still, there had been noise. I'd been alone 10,000 feet high in the mountains on the great Continental Divide, and still there was noise.

Now, in my front yard, in the clear cool dawn, nothing.

I looked up and was instantly humbled.

The heavens were crystal clear, filled with tens of millions of lights . . . souls who had walked this way before, souls who wait to walk this way once more.

I stood there in absolute awe. You could feel the power, the energy of the stillness, of the total silence. So thick it was almost suffocating. It was incredible.

I stood there for five minutes—I swear, five minutes in the darkness—in awe.

There is no doubt in my mind that this kind of energy could never be created by mere man. I felt the power of faith.

I looked to the west and saw the Big Dipper. Turning to the north I thought, it's always darkest before the dawn. Facing east I saw a promise, a soft pink glow on the horizon.

Suddenly, in the distance, softly, ever so softly, I heard "coo coo coo" and though I could not see it, knew it was a beautiful mourning dove.

The bird of peace, I thought as I walked to the house. What a wonderful gift to start the day.

ɛɔ

## No More!

To always have to be right—
is much too excessive
for this excessive man.

# A Sister Sees Her Sister

*"I looked at her," Emma said quietly. "My sister. She was absolutely beautiful, I thought. Two face lifts, breast implants, gorgeous hair."*

Emma paused and looked at me and continued talking.
"My God, she's perfect, I said to myself . . . and she's dead."
You could see pain in Emma's face.
"I was looking at her in the casket after she had committed suicide by driving in front of a train."

Her sister, Emma confided, was the one who had brought her into recovery. Her sister, who had not had a drink in years, started drinking again and had lost her struggle with a deadly disease. A disease that affected her thinking and demanded she be perfect.

Spirit destroyed, her last drink had been moments before she arrived at the railroad tracks.

Perfection—*can* kill!

ళు

## PERFECTION

or the illusion of it—
made my life painful.

In fact,
perfection almost killed me.

That's when I decided
to work real hard at being...

UNPERFECT!

Here's another page for your thoughts.

# Perfect In All My Imperfections

*"The only thing perfect in this world is the word perfect,"*
*I've said many times and believed it. I was wrong.*

"You are Jerry Stanecki," Father Jack said at lunch, "who, throughout your lifetime, has been Jerry Stanecki appropriate, and at times, Jerry Stanecki, inappropriate."

He was right.

What? I'm gonna argue with a priest? That would be most inappropriate!

The difference today is I am not as inappropriate as often as I used to be. Progress, not perfection, that's life.

Eugene O'Neill wrote: "Man is born broken. He lives by mending. The grace of God is glue!"

I believe a little differently. I believe we are all born absolutely perfect instead of broken. How could it be anything less since we come into the universe directly from God?

The imperfection of perfection begins with the very first exposure to all those around us—mother, father, brothers, sisters, teachers, friends—everyone. That healthy ego at birth begins to become diseased. With the love we get we also are given flaws—fear, criticism, cruelty, embarrassment, shame and on and on.

As we grow older we tend to grow inward as fear increases. Fear that we won't be liked for who we are. Fear that what we do won't be good enough. Fear that we'll be rejected, abandoned. I do agree with O'Neill that God is the glue. I also know the glue comes in a lot of different varieties—alcoholism, for example.

I have friends who faced what at first appeared to be the absolute worst admission of their life—admitting they had a problem. Because they accepted the problem and then committed themselves to change, what appeared to be negative found the light of being positive.

You are appropriate, you are inappropriate, you are perfect in your imperfections. Celebrate this. Change what doesn't feel absolutely wonderful. If you don't know how to change, ask, seek out people who have walked the path before you.

I remember the following incident like it happened this morning. We were high in the sacred mountains outside Taos, New Mexico. A rugged, good-looking man in his 60's sat across from me. His face told the story before he did. A story of peace, happiness and satisfaction.

Jean Mayer had come to these mountains in 1958. Dedicated to skiing and spirituality, a force called to him while he lived in Switzerland. He answered the call, came here and found home.

"I know the right way is to lean forward when skiing down the mountain," I said to the ski school founder. "But I'm afraid, and I don't know why."

"That is a natural fear," he said and smiled. "After all, if you're going down a steep mountain, you naturally would hold back, lean back, so not to fall."

"That's it, exactly."

"To deal with that fear, think of the stream that flows on the mountain."

"OK."

"It flows down the mountain, not up . . . effortlessly down. Not so effortlessly if it tries to flow up, huh? So, when you ski down the mountain, lean into it instead of leaning back; welcome, instead of resist. When you do this, you become like the stream flowing effortlessly, without fear."

It worked, and it continues to work in my life today. Life is wonderful, when I lean in—and go with the flow.

∽

# You Are Only As Sick As Your Secrets

*"Were you really raised Catholic?" Randy asked. "Huh?" I replied, wondering where that question came from. "In your column, you wrote about believing you have to struggle and suffer before you can ride off happily into the sunset," Randy explained, "You said that was probably because you were raised Catholic."*

I laughed.

"Yeah, I'm a recovering Catholic." I said. "Now, I can enjoy the pleasure without the guilt."

Randy smiled, looking a little puzzled.

"It's a joke," I explained.

"Oh."

I waited, knowing there was more to come.

"I really related to that," he said. "To feeling guilty."

It was the second time that day someone had mentioned that part of the column.

"That's interesting because a fella named Mayer caught up with me at lunch and said, 'You Catholics are lucky. You're raised with guilt. Jews are born with it.'"

Randy laughed.

Back at work, I was surprised again. A woman named Joy wrote: "You know that business about having to be miserable before you can ride off into the sunset is not owned solely by the Catholics. I was raised Baptist. What a trip to guilt and fear city that was!"

This made me realize that shame is a real killer of the spirit and that many of us have difficulty understanding guilt versus shame.

Here's what helped me. I think John Bradshaw said it.

"Guilt is when you make a mistake. Shame is when you feel that *you* are a mistake."

Think about it.

So many of us were raised hearing comments like "shame on you."

These are cutting, debilitating words that help confuse the meaning of guilt versus shame in young growing minds. Shame is a killer; healthy guilt an asset.

Those thoughts remind me of the most common remark I hear from readers regarding my column.

"You really put yourself out there, Jerry. That takes courage."

At least two dozen people have told me that over the past six months and frankly, it puzzles me.

We all have confusion, fears, challenges and so on. Sharing my faults, my experiences, hopes and strength is a gift for me, because when I give away what helped me—I feel terrific.

I called Mike Kalush, a dear friend who has shared more than a few crises with me. I asked him what he thought people meant by "I put myself out there."

"I think it's that some of us are so inhibited," Mike explained, "that we refuse to show how we really feel. We only show what we want to show. I think when a person goes through a crisis they feel they've got nothing to lose and can display a little weakness." Mike paused and as a second thought added, ". . . or show strength instead of weakness."

Growing, changing, feeling the pain, the joy of little victories is what life is all about for me.

Many of us are taught to keep the secrets, never tell the deep, dark fears. Secrets of self, I believe, seduce you into believing that you are unique and apart—different from everybody else. With that belief, you separate from others, contributing a lack of trust.

The more you withdraw into those secrets, the lonelier you become. The more you hide, the more the fear will grow, like cancer. Before you realize it, all of those secrets have you locked away in a self-created prison.

When I "put myself out there," I set myself free in my spirit.

## HER EGO

**Fred was talking
about a continuing
relationship problem
he was having
with his wife.**

**"The problem is her ego gets
in my way."**

# You stop listening
# when you are ready to talk!

## BE AVAILABLE

# Great Revelations—Not All At Once

*I've been struggling lately, feeling down. I've been unsuccessful in getting work and really cannot figure out what in the world, work-wise, has been going on for the past year.*

I'd been putting a big push on. I cut new video demo tapes, went on auditions, made the rounds at agencies and hundreds of phone calls. Nothing.

One morning, not really wanting to get up, I lay in bed and tried to meditate by listening to my breath going in and out. With every breath I prayed for faith: dear Lord, please give me faith. Over and over, for maybe twenty minutes, I repeated my request for faith, yet the depression stayed.

I know fear is behind the feelings of being alone with no mate or loved one, no daily job with a reward like a weekly paycheck, the frustration of constant rejection. All of that leads to an easy road of continuing depression, self-pity, loneliness, despair.

I struggled, then I jumped on the telephone bright and early and made five calls to prospective jobs. Two were real promising. By the fourth call I had received four rejections in a row. The fifth call I made left me sitting there thinking, well, here's a possible maybe for sure. I laughed.

I started to get bummed but stopped and said to myself, "I know these calls will pay off. What I plant now will grow in the future." I immediately felt better with the way I chose to think. I had became proactive, instead of reactive, to what was happening.

It was an important moment.

The following day I picked up *Today's Gift*, a meditation book that has brought me many gifts.

"There is no magic moment of lasting enlightenment, simply a series of fleeting moments lived one at a time each day. They bring us home to who we've always been."

Wow, I thought, that's sure true but not so easy to consciously recognize. The more I thought about it, the more I realized I seem to learn new behavior as I continue to change, continue to grow.

I realized that by feeling the feelings of rejection from the negative results of phone calls it was OK to be disappointed. However, I also realized that when I decided to be positive and have faith, the crop I plant would grow. I felt better. I had replaced fear with faith and hope.

I had succeeded in starting my day in a proactive way.

∽

## My Way

"Hello, God.
Are you listening to me?"

"The question, my son, is"
came the reply from above,
"are you listening to Me?"

It's hard to hear the message
when you are doing the
talking.

# Look in the Mirror

When your life is not as joyous, happy and free as you'd like it to be—look in the mirror and you'll see the problem!

Once you identify the problem, you can go to work to change.

~

# Understanding Chaos Brings Peace

*This time, I had consciously created the chaos, and like most chaos for me, this one came from fear—concern about money.*

I decided to do some gambling and turned to the stock market. Whoa, Nelly! Talk about chaos, talk about craziness—the rush, the excitement, the "oh nos"—it's all there, as you stare hypnotically at the moving ticker across the bottom of the TV screen.

Are you nuts? I wondered. Yes, sometimes . . . I'm only human.

Dealing with a problem like chaos comes when I recognize it. For me, the problem is there, in the mirror. I am the problem. The realization that self-created obstructions get in the way of enjoying life is the first step to changing the picture. Willingness, willingness to make a change, is the next important step for me.

To get out of my chaos, I needed a walk in the woods.

Come, walk with me.

The path in the snow, from people who had walked here before, makes it easier for us to walk—hmmm, like life.

The sun is bright, the sky deep blue. The tall pines—their limbs weighted with snowy blankets—doze in the warming sun. Listen to the sound of the snow melting off their limbs. Drip, drip, drip.

It's peaceful, especially after the madness of this morning. I had made the decision to bring that chaos into my life. Now, I wanted it out. Getting rid of chaos takes some understanding.

My parents were strong people who, in order for each to feel safe, tried very hard to control each other. The passion of their power struggle came in the form of shouting. That was chaotic, and all of this seemed quite normal to me.

I married, had children, loved them, and was in the process of conditioning them to what I knew when . . . divine intervention occurred. The day I discovered I was addicted to chaos was incredible.

I realized that when things were peaceful, I would not feel safe.

To ease my unsafe feelings, I would stir the pot, and when everything was crazy and chaotic, I would feel safe. I was comfortable with chaos, felt safe in it, because I had learned how to survive, even manipulate, in the chaos.

Today, when I get uneasy with peacefulness, I do a reality check and make the choice not to accept old demons that made me unhappy. Choice. It's powerful.

God, it's beautiful out here. Peaceful, quiet, serene.

Caw, caw, caw, caw, caw.

A half a dozen large crows are going crazy. Screeching, flying in circles, swooping in and out, attacking something at the top of a huge pine tree. I am drawn to the commotion immediately.

I strain to see, I can't see, finally . . . I do see.

It was chaos, and I am here to relax.

I smile and walk away, and with each step the chaos fades.

Understanding, choice, and change . . . what wonderful gifts are available in this fabulous journey called life.

∾

# What Picture Do You Paint Today?

*I am an artist of life—my life. Each day, I try to think of the canvas as blank. What kind of picture do I paint today? The most important brush I use is choice, and choice is a wonderful gift.*

I can choose to paint a reactive, poor me picture. A picture reflecting how I can't seem to get a break, of how unlucky I am or of how the world is against me.

Or, I can paint a proactive picture, one reflecting a positive choice.

*Choice, you have a choice.*

I can be filled with frustration trying to get one of my children to do something, threaten, "If you don't pick that up right now, there will be no cake." Or, "If you don't eat your dinner, there will be no ice cream."

Or, I can choose to be more positive in my approach by saying, "When you get that picked up, I'll give you a piece of cake." Or, "Just as soon as you're finished eating all of your dinner, I'll give you ice cream if you want it, or you can have it later. All you have to do is ask me for it."

Guess which method gets the results.

As a recovering perfectionist, I know one of life's best lessons was the realization I needed to change. Being a perfectionist in an imperfect world, I was a person who would criticize if it wasn't perfect. Insanity? As my friend Junebug Clark would say, "You bet."

✧

"If you take and don't give,
you're a jerk.
I don't want to be a jerk."

-Jim Cash, Screenwriter
1941-2000

# When The Load Gets Heavy

*I woke up at 5:30 one morning feeling rested . . . feeling good. I lay there for maybe 30 seconds before I started to worry. My spirit started to sink as fear, like lava from a volcano, slowly pushed away the good feelings.*

Think differently.

I realized that in my negative thinking I was slipping into a terrible start for the day. I mean, the heavy overcast skies outside were enough to dampen my spirit, let alone feed it with fears of the future.

Yeah, but! My magic magnifying mind screamed. What about the money you owe? What about the house payment? What about no guaranteed money coming in? Freelance work is iffy at times. What about . . . ?

"HEY! THINK DIFFERENTLY!" I jolted myself out of the negative hole I was digging and did a reality check. The house payment isn't due for two weeks. Do I want to waste today and fourteen more days worried about something that is not a demand of today?

THINK DIFFERENTLY!

Yeah, but. I'd been struggling with depression and had kinda boxed myself in. Kinda? I was stuck, obsessing about an old relationship, trying to figure out why it hadn't worked. Sadness and some anger flashed, intensifying the pain of the obsession.

Then I thought about a couple of freelance jobs that had fallen through and was trying to figure out why.

I was frustrated and couldn't figure out why I was having great difficulty writing.

I had exhausted myself with my own insanity. Insanity for me is doing the same thing over and over and expecting different results.

I fought back thinking, this moment is my reality, I have enough money. I have enough food. I have a car, I have gas—in the car. I kept listing what I had.

As crazy as it may seem, I stopped writing and shouted "Thank you God. Thank you for letting me feel better, for letting these words flow. For the feelings I get when the words come." Gratitude sure helps.

I laughed and called my friend Father Jack, a recovering alcoholic priest with 14 years of sobriety—"of the good life," as he puts it.

"Come on over," he said.

Now, I'm not exactly the most comfortable guy in a religious atmosphere. As I sat in the dark wood-paneled lobby of the retreat center waiting, I thought about my yesteryear battles with the nuns of Sacred Heart Grade school.

God, I'd been stubborn and resistant to authority.

"Come on in." The voice interrupted my thoughts. It was Father Jack, he was smiling.

Sitting in his small office with two pictures of a laughing Jesus on the wall, I unloaded. I was feeling hopeless. When I stopped he said, "Think differently."

"Huh?"

"Think differently," he repeated. "Stop trying to figure everything out. You don't have to figure everything out. Give it up and surrender, you're killing yourself."

Think differently! My God, I thought, he's right.

"Yeah, but—I mean, I know where some of the fear comes from. I know what happened when I was a boy that triggers, I know—"

"Jerry," he smiled. "Think differently. Stop trying to figure it out."

"I hear you, thanks."

The lesson was clear. When the negative future started knocking I'd been sucked in until I started to—think differently. Then it all changed—I changed it—I used the power I have.

So, if you're stuck in tomorrow with fear or are having regrets of yesterday, you just might want to—

❧

# First Things First

*"For years," Mary paused, "and I mean years, like two or three, I would say to myself almost every day, I really want to go to college."*

Mary sounded excited, like she had found the final piece of the puzzle. She started getting animated.

"One day, I suddenly realized what I had to do to get what I wanted. I was thrilled."

"What was that?" I asked.

"Register to attend classes." Mary said and laughed.

Mary had learned that taking the action breaks the fear that feeds the procrastination that feeds the fear.

☙

As they say in Hollywood

"ACTION"

for
*Now*
is your chance
of a lifetime!

# Angel in a Snowstorm

*It was cold that Monday morning, bitterly cold, so cold the wind cut through Mary's coat as she hurried from the car into the convenience store. The snow was really starting to come down. Afraid she might not make it later, Mary had rushed to the store to buy a pack of cigarettes.*

Life can be very interesting, as Mary would find out.

She was standing in a checkout line, just before 10 A.M., when she heard the woman next to her ask for a bottle of rum.

"I don't know what compelled me, but I looked at her and I saw myself," Mary told me.

For some reason Mary just couldn't walk away. She really felt a need to talk with the woman. Mary walked around the store trying to think of something to say. The woman walked out the door with her rum and Mary followed. Outside, face to face, Mary asked: "Are you in as much pain as I once was?"

The woman was stunned. "She broke down, and I hugged her."

The woman, named Donna, took a couple of drinks as they sat in Mary's car, engine running for heat. Donna started talking.

"She told me she couldn't stop drinking," Mary said. "She was angry and full of resentment. A lot of people close to her had died in the past few years, including a couple of family members."

Donna drank the rest of the rum trying to kill the emotional pain.

"She said she wanted help," Mary told me. "She asked if I knew anywhere that would take her in."

Mary knew of a few treatment centers but wasn't sure if the woman's insurance was good. Mary told Donna she'd drive her home to check her insurance. Donna refused, and drove herself home. A drunk is sometimes hard to get through to.

At the house Mary found that the closest treatment center the woman's insurance would cover was in a town 35 miles away. A call to the facility brought a "we can't help today" answer. Mary persisted, Donna was desperate. The voice on the phone told Mary she could talk to the "big guy," the boss. Mary drove the 35 miles. One look and the "big guy" told Mary to take Donna to the hospital.

"Oh my God, what have I gotten myself into?" Mary chuckled, recalling her thoughts. "By this time, she's starting to tell me she wants to go home. Oh, God, I said a few prayers. My dad was an alcoholic and it brought back so many memories of me as a child, and the fears. Finally, I told her, I've come this far for help and that she was right where she was supposed to be that day."

With Donna safely admitted to the hospital, Mary stopped at the woman's house and told her husband what had happened.

"He was just totally amazed that I could get her to go. I told him I didn't do anything, she was asking for help. He was so kind and grateful."

It was after seven that night when Mary finally got home to her family, some ten hours after she had gone to the store. She felt good, tired, but good.

It's said Angels come in different packages. I don't know about that.

What I do know is it's a good thing this angel is one who smokes.

# She Died Thursday—Courage Doesn't Come Easy

*It was a story a friend was starting to tell about an experience with "wants" versus "needs." It was a life experience he'd heard at a support group meeting.*
*"But," I protested, "aren't you violating anonymity rules if you tell me?"*

He explained that the story would not violate the anonymity because he'd changed the names and place. He felt it was a powerful example of a problem a lot of folks struggle with and that it was important to share the story.

The problem? Sometimes it's real hard to distinguish between "wanting" something versus "needing" something.

"My needs are always met," my friend said. "My wants are what get me into trouble." We sat there, drinking a cup of coffee, as he told the story of a young man struggling to stay sober, and a middle-aged man with purpose in his life.

He was a 22-year-old with the killer good looks of a young Brando. He was shaking slightly as he sat at the table in the basement of a church. Black hair, lean, dark eyes filled with anxiety, this young man had found his way to the table on a cold October Saturday night.

"My name is Mike, I'm an addict. I don't usually come to this meeting because I usually go to a younger group. I'm here tonight because I really want to drink, I mean, I feel it in my heart. I worked 100 hours this week, and I just want to go out and drink until I pass out."

Mike said he had been straight and sober for six months . . . this time. Twice before he had relapsed, and the last time he had made a promise to himself to stay straight, but promises are easily broken when it comes to addiction.

"A couple of friends called and asked me to go out drinking," Mike said, "but I told them I might meet them later. Instead I came here because I'm so afraid."

My friend said he felt an immediate need to tell the kid that he, Mike, was winning—winning, because he was here, and more importantly he was recognizing the fear. It was the fear of not being in the present. It was fear that he would fail. Sometimes it's hard to see the tree from the forest.

A few more people shared their story and it came around to a man old enough to be Mike's father.

"My name is Dick, I'm an alcoholic. I remember Mike, when I was six months sober. That was seven years ago. I was six months sober and the doctors told me I had cancer. But I didn't drink over it.

"A few months later, as I was recovering from an operation, a moving van pulled up in front of my house, and my wife of 24 years packed everything into it and left me. I didn't drink over that."

My friend says you could hear a pin drop.

"Two years ago I met a woman in this program and found what I had been looking for all my life. She gave me unconditional love and taught me how to give unconditional love. It's like these tables, there's love here, people don't judge you here."

Dick talked quieter now.

"Last August first, we were on vacation when she turned yellow. A short time later she was diagnosed with pancreatic cancer." Dick paused to gather his emotions. "Two days ago, she died in my arms . . . I didn't drink over that."

Dick looked directly at Mike.

"Mike—you don't have to drink either."

Power. There is, without doubt, incredible power at these tables of strangers who are intimate before they meet. Strangers, who come believing they are different, unique, and that no one has their problems. Yet these brothers and sisters-in-arms sit next to each other and share their secrets, experiences, and hopes, and are surprised with the realization that the person next to them is not talking about your secrets, but their own, and *theirs* are yours.

Power and strength constantly remind us that life really doesn't get better. Bad things still happen, but YOU get better. It reminds you that alone, it is almost impossible, but together nothing is impossible.

I can't—we can.

❧

# Hi In The Sky

*"I'm still pissed that my mother died and it's been three years." Chris was talking about her anger. "On the date of the first anniversary I planned to stay home, telling myself I couldn't deal with work, you know, I had a day of 'poor me' all planned."*

"I was in the shower when it happened," Chris continued. "It was about 9:15 in the morning and I was remembering that Mom died about ten in the morning when suddenly I heard this voice. I mean it was clear as can be. It said, 'When are you going to stop feeling sorry for Chris and start feeling happy for your mother?' I swear, it was that clear."

Chris got out of the shower and went to work. She felt better than she had in a year.

Later, Chris went to a baseball game her son was playing in.

Sitting in the stands, Chris began thinking about how her mom always loved watching her kids and then her grandkids at play.

"So I was thinking, OK, Mom, if you're there do something, show me a sign." Chris paused. "And you know what, my son hit a grand slam homerun.

"I was stunned and I looked up into the sky to, you know, say thanks and I swear, as God as my judge, there in the sky was the word 'Hi!' I mean it was as clear as day—even my daughter saw it.

"Today, when I'm hurting, I need to remember those *God* moments."

℘

# SURRENDER

**When you stop
using force,
when you stop resisting—**

**you find
Power**

# The Power from Surrender

*A woman in Oprah Winfrey's audience asked if she should give up on trying to accomplish her dream. The woman knew she had great talent, but said her problem was others didn't realize it. She was frustrated and feeling hopeless.*

Oprah answered by telling the story of how she got the role of Sofia in the movie *The Color Purple*.

"I'd never wanted anything—anything—as much in my life as that role," Oprah explained.

At the time, Oprah said, she didn't know Steven Spielberg or Quincy Jones, two key players behind production of the film. She fretted until someone suggested she audition for the part. Forcing herself to push through the doubt and fear, Oprah read for it.

Two months passed with Oprah just short of having conniption fits because she wanted that role so badly. Finally, patience worn thin, she called the casting agent.

"What you don't realize," the casting director told her in what sounded like a not-too-sympathetic voice, "is there are other actresses auditioning for the part."

Hearing the list of actresses who'd read for the part, Oprah felt like it was all over—she'd never get the role.

Discouraged, she checked into a health spa. She worked hard there, not only trying to win the constant battle she has with weight, but to stop obsessing over the film role.

Oprah persisted until finally her moment of truth came. She realized that if she didn't surrender all of her emotional turmoil from wanting something so badly, she was only going to become more anxious, more miserable, more unhappy.

"I'll never forget this," Oprah said. "I'm gonna cry—I was out-side running on the track singing the song, 'I Surrender' when I truly *did* surrender. I said, 'God, what's your will?'

"The moment I surrendered, I swear, someone came running out and shouted, 'Stephen Spielberg is on the phone for you.' Spielberg said he heard I was at a fat farm, and if I lost one pound I'd lose the part."

The rest of the story—the rave reviews, the power of Oprah's performance, and the message delivered—is history.

When we truly admit our helplessness and—with honesty of the heart—*surrender*, we are given the *power*.

Listening to Oprah tell her story that day, I felt a chill. Goose bumps covered both of my arms.

I've been there—where Oprah was that day in a place and time where all is still and relief comes with surrender. I've celebrated the victory and received *the power* that came from *surrender*. But, it wasn't always that way.

In the yesterdays of my life, before I was touched by the grace of a power so much greater than I, my feelings about Oprah's story would have been, that's nice, but she's crazy—you never win when you give up.

Time flies, people change—sometimes. Life has taught a lot of us that only when we hurt enough do we reach the point of no re-turn—we either surrender or stay locked in the misery.

Twenty or so years ago, I sat in the living room of an old Victo-rian mansion in a decaying section of downtown Detroit. I had come to visit with a grizzled, hockey-playing, fire-truck-driving, former two-fisted drinking Catholic priest who ran a drug and al-cohol treatment center.

I had done a story for television on this priest, Father Vaughn Quinn, and we'd become friends. This cold November evening, we sat across from each other discussing the mystery of life.

"Jerry, don't you realize God gives you the gift of pain to bring about change?" Quinn asked in a husky, whiskey-cured voice laced with a slight Irish brogue.

"You're nuts," I told him. Such arrogance I displayed . . . such ignorance.

I realize now that I didn't know any better then. But I, like Quinn, was a tough guy and as far as I was concerned, pain came with the territory. Pain sure didn't bring *me* any "time to change" messages.

It didn't take long for me to begin to realize the truth in Quinn's words. It was only when my pain got so great . . . *too* great, that I became willing to begin a journey of change.

℘

What do you need to surrender? Willingness! Please feel free to write your thoughts below.

# Do You Appreciate Yourself?

*"Do you appreciate you? I mean, really appreciate who you are?" Willie, my pal, asked. Interesting question, isn't it? It's especially interesting when you hear the second part of Willie's question. "Do you like yourself enough to play?"*

Fascinating, I thought, he was really talking about self-esteem.

"Do you like you enough to take care of yourself when you're stressed out?" Willie asked. "Do you play?"

"Yeah, sure," I answered, kind of evasively.

"How much do *you* play?" I asked, trying to turn the worm and avoid the rest of the conversation, which is something I do when I get uncomfortable about me.

"Why are you sidestepping the question, Jerry?"

"I guess because it's making me uncomfortable."

Later, thinking about the idea of play I again shifted from me to someone else. A friend who works in the auto industry.

Bill is 51 and I don't know how he's made it this long. Bill's job is high stress, fast and high profile. He's a Type A personality. A perfect candidate, I thought, for a quadruple bypass.

"I don't think I know the meaning of play, let alone do it," Bill said honestly.

I felt compassion for Bill, who needs to play more. But it's hard to play when you're feeling afraid you might not be evaluated as worthwhile by the boss.

What's that? You relate to my pal and you'd like an example of play? Good for you. That's the first step, the willingness to want to change by understanding. I applaud you.

For me play comes in all forms. A lot of the time it's laughing at myself even for a couple of minutes. At other times it's the joy of my eccentricities.

When I'm feeling the pressures of being a recovering Type A personality—when I work too hard and obsess over the work too much—I walk.

At times I'd catch myself still gritting my teeth, racking my brain, and wondering why my shoulders are so tight—that would be a mile or so into the walk.

Usually, a gift from the universe like a crow cawing or the slurping and thrashing of carp feeding in frenzy along the banks of the lake help me snap out of it.

As I make progress taking care of myself, I catch my intensity.

One winter day, I was almost through my walk when I realized I hadn't taken one deep breath. I came out of the woods and looked at the field. A foot of snow covered the ground.

There was a trampled path around the field where others had walked. Me? I chose to walk across the untouched snow making footprints—the mark of man on this canvas.

Ten steps—twenty. The sky got bluer, the spotty clouds, whiter. My mind flashed on a deserted beach, of thoughts of Swiss Family Robinson . . . and then shifted to the poem *Footprints In The Sand.*

Stopping and looking behind me, I saw my tracks and laughed. Carefully I turned in place and started walking in the same direction I had been—only backwards. The thought of someone following my track from the woods, then reaching mid-field to meet tracks coming from the other way delighted me.

They wouldn't know if I was coming or going.

I took a deep breath, then another. It was amazing. When I started walking—thinking I was playing—I was deceiving myself. I really wasn't playing or relaxing because I was thinking about work and other things that troubled me.

Once I recognized I was not playing, that I didn't know if I was coming or going, I could choose to change. When I flashed on the silly idea of walking forward, then backward—I had won.

Laugh at yourself. Appreciate you for you. Play is powerful.

❧

# Traffic Problems Can be Food for the Soul

*"My God, every road in this town is under construction,"*
*Dylan said. "It's enough to make you want to kill*
*someone." Thinking twice about what he'd said and*
*considering the times we live in, he added, "And the sad*
*thing is people are losing control to road rage and are*
*killing each other."*

"Or, in the very least, there's a lot of 'You're number one' salutes and plenty of ill manners," I said.

"You always try to be positive. What's positive about driving, or trying to, in all the construction?" Dylan asked.

When negative things happen to me, I quickly try to see what the exact nature of my thinking is. If it's reactive and self-defeating thinking based on old habits, I try to change right then and there.

The traffic on the freeway had come to a halt. Surrounded by orange barrels, the reflectors on the top of each barrel reflected how I felt—resentful.

Let's see, I thought, turning off the radio to limit my distractions. How am I really feeling and how is it affecting my happiness and what can I choose to do about it now?

I'm impatient, that's for sure, so what can I do to change that? I can consciously be patient. Duh, I laughed.

As I thought more about the situation I was in, I saw tremendous opportunity in being in this traffic mess. This could be a valuable lesson for me.

Am I angry? Hell yes, but acceptance takes away the anger. How about rejection of others? Woo boy, I just edged out the car next to me to get ahead to go nowhere. Hello! Impulsive? Yup. Egotistic?

That's why I'm in front of him. How do I change? I share and I do: I pause to let another driver go ahead of me.

How about jealousy? Envy? False pride? Am I jealous of the woman who is past the construction? (Be grateful for what I have.) Envious of her? (Be happy in the good fortune of others.) Think it should be me because I'm more important? Ego, false pride, arrogance . . . ah, seems to fit. Need to change—humility.

In the arena of beating myself up, let's see, "If I would have been as smart as I think I am (perfect) I wouldn't be feeling inadequate (rejection of self), or like a victim (get honest, this is just life) for procrastinating (take action now—thinking about this is taking positive action) and not being able to make a decision (indecisiveness) to take another route."

Or, how about worry? "I just know if I don't get there I will lose the sale." Counter that with, "She'll understand, everybody knows the nightmare of road construction, it's been all over the news."

These are just a few of the thoughts that came to me and you know what? I really felt a lot better about me.

Instead of freaking out, making myself insane, miserable and unhappy, I had used the time to better understand me . . . and the more I understand myself, the more I am in control of the only thing in this world I do control . . . me.

I pulled past the last barrel and slammed my foot on the accelerator. In seconds, I was flying at 80 m.p.h. Then it hit me. I'd just gone through this terrific process in balancing my thoughts, in restoring my peacefulness and within seconds I was right back into old habits. I slowed down and felt better.

Yup, old habits die hard, especially it seems with the pressure and stress of living in today's world.

The last gift from the construction experience was to realize I can use any opportunity to feed the soul, for when the spirit soars the mind will follow.

❧

# When 'What if's' Turn Positive

*"If I start getting really weird, really crazy while you're here, it's because of the trial." My friend Frannie's voice came over the long distance line from San Francisco.*

Frannie sounded frightened. "I get real nervous and have an anxiety attack just thinking about it and can't do anything about it."

My first impulse was to say, "Frannie, you can do something about the anxiety now," but I didn't. Even though I believe 10,000% that we can manage our thoughts and energy, I didn't feel like Frannie needed to be told by me what to do.

Frannie was talking about a visit I was planning that would coincide with a court date she had . . . a court date six weeks away.

Through no fault of her own, she'd been injured in a plane accident that caused her long-term pain, and finally surgery. The physical pain was compounded by emotional terror from lawyers, depositions and accusations. Everyone had attacked Frannie, saying she was at fault. Right! It was Frannie who, from seat 34-A, slammed on the brakes of the jet while taxiing down the runway.

Thinking of the best way to be supportive I said, "Frannie, I understand completely what you're saying and feeling, and appreciate very much your concern about my visit. Don't worry, it'll be just fine."

She was clearly stressed.

"Frannie, do you think you might be afraid because you might not get what you want?" I asked.

"No," she answered quickly, "it's not that. It's just that the man from the airline—a young attorney—said some really hurtful things."

"It sounds like you're taking what he said personally."

"Well, it is," she answered.

I explained that, for me, it's a personal attack if I choose to allow it. It is not personal, however, if I choose to believe it's just another attorney saying what he's got to say to try save his own butt, save his client money, and help them avoid responsibility.

A key tool used by attorneys in situations like this is to imply, suggest, even flat out accuse. Why not just say, "Shame on you! You bad person!"

Gimme a break. Give yourself a break.

Today, I absolutely refuse to allow anyone to shame me, blame me, use me, in order to avoid accepting responsibility for their actions. This is a big part of my responsibility in taking care of me, in changing old pictures that made me a victim.

Today, when fear, anxiety and panic come knocking on my door, the very first thing I consciously think of is, "I am afraid I am not going to get what I want." That's it—the bottom line. We all want what we want, when we want it.

If I want to stay peaceful and fear-free, I remember the Rolling Stones song: "You can't always get what you want, but if you try—you just might get what you need."

"Try" for me is trust—trust in the universe, in God.

When I choose to replace the fear with trust and belief that what happens will be the very best for me, I win.

Instead of a day filled with fear, worry, anger, resentment, self pity, shame, etc., my day—which is all I really have—becomes a day of play.

For me, that trust and faith brings gratitude for the wisdom to know the difference.

It's all very easy to say, and for me, sometimes very, very hard to execute. But I have proven over and over that surrender to trust and faith is not losing, not failure . . . but absolute joyous victory.

෴

# It Takes a Real Man to Say 'I Was Wrong'

*Funny how resentments die hard. Actually, not so funny, for resentment is being unhappy about someone, or something, that has hurt or insulted us. The killer part of resentment is re-feeling the hurt. Re-feeling the hurt . . . sometimes for a long time, and the person who hurt you doesn't even know you still feel the pain. Or do they?*

An amazing thing happened during one of the 1999 Super Bowl pre-game shows.

Former Pittsburgh quarterback, now broadcaster, Terry Bradshaw did a report on Thomas "Hollywood" Henderson, a guy Bradshaw didn't like.

Twenty years earlier—*twenty*—Bradshaw and Henderson were on opposing teams for Super Bowl XIII, Dallas versus Pittsburgh. During the pre-game hype, Henderson said Bradshaw wasn't the smartest quarterback around. He said Bradshaw couldn't spell "cat," even if he was spotted the "C" and "T."

That hurt Bradshaw so deeply that, years later when he was inducted into the Hall of Fame, he talked about it. Henderson, who by then had blown his football career with drugs and alcohol, was in prison.

During the Bradshaw interview, Henderson talked about life now, fifteen years clean and sober. He talked about how he works for the community he lives in, helping build a football field and field house for kids. That's today.

"When I played football, I never thought about philanthropy, service, family. I was a selfish, self-centered drug addict," Henderson said. "I've been sober fifteen years, and what's become important to me is family, community, philanthropy, giving. The more I give the better I feel."

Bradshaw looked at Henderson, now twenty years later, and said sarcastically, "Cat, K-A-T." Resentments die hard.

Henderson laughed and the two settled down to talk.

Bradshaw asked if, back then, Henderson knew he was hurting his team. Did he care? Henderson answered, as an honest man would, and said at the time, he didn't care. Addiction can do that to you. Dallas lost the game of games. Henderson lost a career, and almost his soul.

Then, the amazing part of this story happened. Henderson told how he was in prison watching Bradshaw's induction into the Hall of Fame on TV. Out of all the things Bradshaw could have talked about, he talked about a fool in Dallas who had said he couldn't spell *cat*.

Henderson recalled lying in his cell and promising himself, "if there ever comes a day, there's an eighth and ninth step I wanna take."

Then, during the interview, Henderson looked directly into Bradshaw's eyes and said firmly, gently: "I want to make amends to you. I shouldn't have done it, and it was wrong for me to do it. So one more time in my life, I'm able to work out something and say I was wrong to do it."

Bradshaw was shocked. Henderson put his hand out, Bradshaw shook it, and said, "It takes a big man to say I'm sorry."

Thomas Henderson was referring to the eighth and ninth steps of the 12-step Alcoholic Anonymous program, which simply says, when you do something to hurt someone, admit your wrong and make amends, as long as it doesn't do further harm.

It's amazing what honesty with self . . . and a little help from friends, can bring about.

The misconception is that if you're wrong, you're bad, less than, or just dumb. It's undesirable to be wrong. Or is it?

"Terry," Henderson said, "I've come to the place now where I am *not* my mistakes, I'm not my past; I *am* who I become today."

# In the Darkness, a Cardinal Sings of Faith

*It was just after six one morning when it happened. "Ta-ree, ta-ree, ta-ree." I smiled, for it was the first sign of spring. In the darkness of the dawn, I visualized the red cardinal who was calling the day into play.*

It was the first time this year, I realized, that I'd heard birds sing in the predawn.

The cardinal had faith, I thought. Faith that the darkness would disappear, and the light of day would bring newness and change. Faith is powerful.

I had lain in bed half asleep, floating in and out of what I planned to write about. I'd been struggling, the night had been restless as I worried about money and bills due.

Get back to now, Jerry, I said to myself. Today, on the money issue you're OK, you're not broke today. Stay in the now, focus on what to write. I was trying, but it wasn't happening. I got up feeling frustrated.

I decided I would change my morning routine. Instead of getting up, making coffee and reading the newspaper, I would do it differently. I would get up, make coffee, meditate and pray, then write before I read the paper.

I had come to the conclusion that by reading the newspaper I was polluting my creativeness, and that was the least of it.

The black and white print telling me of man's inhumanity to man, of violence, death, destruction, of cruelty, was taking me down, way down, yet I found it seductive. I found myself resisting change, which I guess is just human nature.

I was determined to bring the positive into my life before the negative.

Maybe I'll have one cup of coffee, and read just the front page, I thought, heading out the front door to walk to the road to get the paper. I was already working against my good intentions because I had decided to leave the paper in the drive until I had written.

Taking a deep breath, I looked at the clouds. Another gray day, a Monday gray day. Monday gray days used to be killers for me because I would really feel worthless.

My mind, my magic magnifying mind, would tell me—no, scream at me—that there was something wrong with me because I was the only one in the world, it seemed, who wasn't going to a job that Monday morning.

Feelings of guilt, rejection, shame, all ganged up on me, I would feel terrible.

I have never quite figured out what that was all about, but I have taken action to change that thinking. I realize now and am grateful for the gift I have been given. I realize now that my needs are continually met, more than I could imagine in past fear. I also know that my wants get me in trouble.

I wanted to read the paper. I needed to change my morning routine.

Yet I wanted what I wanted, when I wanted it. Sound familiar? I glanced at the front page, tempting myself, kinda like I'll just eat one potato chip. I started to pour a cup of coffee but stopped.

Was that what I thought it was? It was. I ran out on the back deck and looked up, searching. Then I saw them, hundreds of geese, two giant, wiggling dancing lines shaped in a V high in the sky, and they were headed north. I took a deep breath, then another, and watched the geese dissolve into the clouds. At that moment, I was filled with how good my life is. I'd found the secret to success in life . . . it's to enjoy the journey.

"Ta-ree, ta-ree, ta-ree" the cardinal sang. It sounded like, Jer-rey, Jer-rey, Jer-rey, spring's coming. Spring, what a wonderful part of the gift of life.

ço

# It's There. All You Have to Do is See It

*"Dad, I'm really worried."* It was my 21-year-old daughter, Anastasia, calling from Florida where she lives. Words like that tend to concern a father. "What's this about?"

"I'm going to school, I'm working, but I feel like I'm running out of time to be somebody, make something of my life."

I smiled.

"Honey, when you're 80 that will be a justified fear."

"I'm serious, Dad."

I reassured my daughter, saying that what she was feeling was absolutely normal for young women and men trying to figure out their purpose in life. Hell, I'm more than twice her age and still don't know what I want to be. We talked a while longer and Annie said she felt better.

Just as it is the little things that cause so many problems when you think too much about them, it's the little things that cause so much joy—when you let them.

Life has always had to be so serious for me, and I so perfect. I always had to figure "it" out. Whatever "it" was.

The universe has been very interesting.

One morning, I needed to walk. In the woods at Cranbrook, a parklike private school, I turned my face into the sun, felt the warmth and inhaled the smell of pine that filled the air.

I smiled at the memory of Annie's dilemma and thought, sometimes the simplest question is the most profound. A question like: what's the purpose of my life? "Not too heavy," I said to myself and laughed.

Suddenly, I heard music. Following the sound, I climbed a hill and came upon a small outdoor amphitheater. A bearded man was playing the piano and singing the words, "Just the good."

The stage was covered with children, maybe 8, 9, 10 years old. The beard sang, "Just the good," then paused to let the children try the line.

"Just the good," they sang in broken harmony followed by giggles and laughter.

Another man, a large—well, fat man—holding a music book up at nose level, peered through glasses balanced delicately on his nose and sang the line in a high, almost falsetto voice.

Something told me this man was no stranger to people who could, and sometimes did, laugh at such a big man with such a high voice.

Yet, here he was, singing his heart out, giving to the children, some who appreciated it and others who probably did not.

He had found his purpose in his life, not as a great Metropolitan Opera singer, but as a teacher of children. He was experiencing purpose, he seemed happy. This is what life is all about, I thought, because by giving unconditionally, without expecting anything in return, you get pure joy.

I realized that all the giving I've done in life, with my family, with my job on television, was always with the feeling that I deserved no thanks, that I was just doing my job. The job I was conditioned to do from birth, to take care of others, have all the answers, fix all, and expect nothing in return, was fine except I was in pain and sadly realized I had lost my way.

I continued to walk, still asking what's my purpose in life? Then I saw him, the old man, sitting on a patch of dirt. Amazingly, he was pulling weeds, one weed at a time. I was shocked. Hadn't this fellow heard of weed killer?

Wanting to ask him why in the world he was doing it that way, I hesitated. He looked like he was in deep thought. What's he thinking, I thought, walking past him, determined not to disturb him with what he might think is a dumb question. I walked a little further and just couldn't stand it. My insatiable curiosity got the best of me.

As I approached, he didn't look up; he just kept pulling one weed at a time. Weed after weed after weed.

"Excuse me," I asked, "I hope I'm not intruding, but are you practicing patience?"

"Nope, just sittin' on my ass."

We laughed, and he told me he had been thinking about financial planning, his work for 35 years. But his main thought, he said, was in getting the weeds pulled and the flowers planted.

"But one weed at a time?" I asked.

"Yup." He answered, needing to say no more, for his look of relaxed peace said it all.

He had a three year plan, he said, for this garden, so when people came out of church they would see beauty instead of blah.

Plan the future, but not the outcome, I thought as I walked away.

The secret, the purpose of existing, is in staying in today, in the moment, in celebrating the wonderful gifts the universe offers each moment for NOW is my chance of a lifetime.

It's NOW that I can choose to sing the songs of peace and acceptance, instead of struggle and disappointment.

It all felt good, I felt good, filled with deep gratitude. All because I chose to be available to receive all the gifts of this day. It's there, I thought, it's all there—you only have to see it.

ca

# Celebrate

# Your

# Spirit!

# Gifts from the Universe—Make Yourself Available

*Sometimes, I find myself struggling over little things, such as what is the meaning of life or what are we here for.*

Feeling stressed and a little lost, I had gone for a walk and had found wonderful examples of purpose in life, of just being.

I'd found children—part of a theater group—singing, and their teacher teaching. He'd found purpose.

I went back looking for the music, but instead I found death.

Coming out of the woods and into a meadow I saw 20 or so Canada geese feeding peacefully on the side of a hill.

Suddenly my eye caught movement. It was a dog, a ratty looking terrier racing down the hill. Stretched fully, tail wagging, focus in his eyes, he ran toward the geese. He was on a mission.

The geese panicked and started running. RUNNING, instead of flying. Within seconds—the little terrier, which looked much like Orphan Annie's dog—had caught a goose. Biting at it, he knocked the goose down into the dirt.

"HEY!" I shouted, clapping my hands loudly trying to scare the dog. "HEY!" Running toward the goose I shouted again. "HEY! GET, DOG!" He didn't even look up.

Just as suddenly as the first dog appeared, a big black dog ran down the hill, but didn't seem to notice the struggle.

As suddenly as he had come, the terrier was gone. Distracted by the other dog now running into the woods, the ratty killer, without a second look at its prey, bounced happily off into the woods as though nothing had happened.

When I reached the wounded goose, it just laid there, legs shaking, twitching, I imagine, from pain.

"Why didn't you fly?" I asked. She just looked at me.

Softly, with my fingertips, I rubbed the crown of her head. I felt her long neck. It seemed OK. I rolled her over and saw blood, although not much, under the left wing.

As I stroked her back softly she lifted her head and placed it in the palm of my other hand. Quietly, she lay there, seemingly grateful for the gentleness.

She was so beautiful, silent and still, not afraid. I sat there silently for what seemed like five minutes, all the time softly stroking her. Her eyes stayed locked on mine. Then slowly she closed her eyes for the last time and the shade of death, a glasslike film, came over them. It had been a long time since I'd seen death so intimately.

Why didn't you fly, I wondered again sadly, and realized that if she was meant to fly, she would have flown. This time, her time, she wasn't supposed to fly.

Not having anything to dig a grave, I picked a yellow day lily and placed it on her and walked away, hoping the groundskeeper would find her soon and give her a proper burial.

I walked toward the art museum, thinking about the natural rhythm of the universe and what I had just been a part of. I was sad, yes, yet I was filled with acceptance. This is what is.

I washed my hands in the fountain of Orpheus in front of the museum, a fountain created by sculptor Carl Milles. Four bronze women, three men, listening to music, singing the song of life—and death. A song I had just experienced.

I walked down the stairs and under a long row of chestnut trees and wondered: Do chestnut trees grow in the desert?

◌

Feed your soul daily,

for when the spirit soars,
the mind follows!

When fear knocks at the
door—
answer it with faith
and there will be no one
there.

# Someday—If You Pay Attention, Can Be Today

*I stood there in the open doorway, aiming at the kitten. Happy—that was her name—was standing half in and half on top of the snow as she tried to figure out why she couldn't be completely on top. I aimed and fired.*

Once, twice, and a third shot.

As I put the camera away, I thought someday when I'm old I'll sit in a chair, look at the picture, and remember the joy Happy, the cat, gave me. Then, it hit me. Someday? Someday? What's wrong with today?

I'm sure you've heard the expression, "This is not a dress rehearsal," well, that's what went through my mind as I planned for "someday."

"Work hard, study hard, and someday you'll be rich and famous," I remember hearing as a boy. So I did. I worked hard and long, and was successful, and I had a taste of the fame, so to speak.

Happy? Nope, because the "someday" caused a lot of problems that I couldn't quite figure out.

Believe it or not, it took forty years, a tremendous amount of pain, a little help from professionals and a lot of help from friends to realize the "someday" was a huge roadblock in my happiness.

I finally understood that "someday" meant my reward for all that hard work was always around the corner, always just out of reach, always coming someday, which never comes. Get it?

I worked for years without feeling worthy enough for a reward, such as a vacation. I'd tell myself I'll take the vacation when I deserved it, when I was successful, someday. Getting the drift?

What this belief did was throw gasoline on the insane fires I had for perfection, perfection at any cost. I remember working in television news in the days we used film. My stories were long for television news, 6-10 minutes long, and each part of the story, like a sound bite, was on a separate reel of film.

I'd take four, maybe five reels of film to a director where projectors would be loaded, each with a different reel. We'd then mix all the footage into the finished story by switching from one reel/projector to another. If a cue was missed, or timing was off, we'd have to do it all over.

I was so insane, so much of a perfectionist, that one day as we reached the end of the mixed piece, eight minutes and 50 seconds into the mix, with just ten seconds left, I saw a single black grease mark on the film. A grease mark! If you blinked, you'd miss the grease mark. But, for me, the perfectionist, it wasn't good enough. It had to be fixed. Let's do it again, I told the director. Insanity? I think so today. I'd like to say that was a rare occasion, but truth is, things like that happened quite a bit. All because of my perfectionism and pride. I'm sure those guys in master control hated to see me coming.

Today, I feel now is my chance of a lifetime. Today, now, I can watch and enjoy the play of a little kitten. Today, not someday.

Standing in the doorway watching Happy play in the snow, I realized how much I appreciate who I am today, and how I can enjoy a less than perfect existence. I realized I was feeling—happy.

കൃ

# Kindness—Sometimes Forgotten, Still Lasts a Lifetime

*The eight-year-old boy was playing inside a friend's house when, for no particular reason, he started singing.*

"You have a very nice voice." Mrs. Housefeld said to the little boy from across the street. "You sing wonderfully."

The boy felt terrific, and sang with even more spirit.

Kindness came to mind this morning. Why, I don't really know, but just the thought of kindness makes me feel good. Somebody doing or saying something that makes you feel cared for, wanted, appreciated . . . worth more.

Criticism, on the other hand, one word of it, can blow out the last flicker of the flame.

Kindness is encouragement that can spark the wildfire within that brings greatness.

I grew up in a neighborhood of pre-World War II bungalow houses on Swain Court, in Milwaukee, Wisconsin. It was a street where you knew everybody.

Sometimes, kindness comes in unusual ways.

I remember when I was about four years old, each day I would run to the corner of Swain Court and Ohio streets. It was only 50 feet or so from the house, but for a four-year-old it was a big adventure.

On the corner, I would sit and wait anxiously for the old man with three thumbs.

He would come down the street, walking slowly from the streetcar stop.

Blue work shirt spotted with dirt, he'd be carrying his black metal lunch pail, looking like he'd had a hard day at the factory.

The closer he got, the more excited I became. I would shout, "Mister, Mister please Mister, show me, show me."

No matter how tired the old man might be, he would stop, smile, stoop down and show me his right hand.

There they were!

I stared in amazement at two thumbs on one hand. One thumb looked normal, except out of the side of it grew another thumb. It was incredible, and to a four-year-old boy born curious as a kitten, it was like seeing the seventh wonder of the world.

"How'd you do that? How'd you do that?" I would ask.

He would smile and say, "A gift from God, my little friend. A gift to make your day exciting."

I felt unbelievably wonderful.

He would ask me about my day. He cared about it, about me. We would talk for a few minutes, and he'd be on his way.

What a wonderful old man.

What a wonderful gift his kindness was.

Starting today, and each day from now on, I promise to take a moment and remember the old man with three thumbs, and his kindness. I promise to make an extra special effort to think a little less about me and my needs, and take time to give some kindness away.

Funny how sometimes kindness and those warm memories get misplaced—but never forgotten.

Oh, one more thing. More than forty years later, that singing boy still remembers the warm, loving feeling he had when he was told he sang well—and I still think I can't sing very well at all. But I sure remember Mrs. Housefeld's kindness.

♋

# Want More from Life? Less Can be More

*It was just after seven on a beautiful but cool spring morning. Bouncer, my calico cat, was sitting in the window staring outside. "Do you want to go out there?" She looked at me and got up. I opened the sliding glass door and she ran quickly out into the winter-stilled rose garden. Spring was here; she was hunting.*

It was time for the chipmunks to yawn, stretch and crawl out of a winter bed of leaves and twigs. Bouncer was ready, sitting on the stone wall, hind legs cocked under, ready to spring into action. Her head up, still as a statue, she was waiting, watching.

Imagine the chipmunks' thoughts: "First time out this year and look what I run into?"

When I first moved here, Bouncer would knock off a chipmunk a day.

At first she'd proudly bring it to the door. Cats do that. As time passed, she got complacent. Forget about bringing them to Daddy—just chow down.

By June of each year, her interest fades; at times, she falls asleep on watch. A testy little chipmunk boldly runs right in front of her nose, unseen.

By August, old Bouncer just sits there, awake, watching as the chipmunks do whatever they want. Bouncer ignores them, she's had her fill.

Soon the leaves drop from the trees and the first snowfall sends the chipmunks to sleep another winter away. Bouncer strolls to the front of the fire and falls asleep.

Funny how life works for Bouncer. The more she has, the less she wants. But, then, that's how life works.

I wondered about the natural rhythm of life and the universe—about wants and needs, and how when I try to force something I push it away. But, when I embrace it, it comes to me.

In 1983 I decided I would try to do whatever I wanted to, whenever I wanted, and see if I could survive. Scary? Absolutely. But one of the advantages of being me was that I didn't know better.

Over the past seventeen years, I've created a couple of television shows, written a book, acted in movies, demolished and rebuilt a house from scratch, and traveled to rebel territory in the jungles of Guatemala to produce a video about American doctors and nurses on a mercy mission.

Oh, I also broke my neck, had a heart attack and quintuple bypass open heart surgery. Life has been good.

What's truly amazing is that without having the security of a "job," not only have I survived, but the quality of my life just kept getting better and better. I never had a lot of money, but my needs have been met beyond my expectations.

How? As time passed, my fear-based expectations faded as I realized my needs were being taken care of. As I developed more faith in my God and universe, my expectations were gradually replaced by acceptance. Eventually, trust and faith took the place of expectations.

The less I wanted, the more I received—check that: the more I receive in quality of living.

Want change in your life? Willingness and trust is the beginning that makes anything possible.

❧

## NEEDS AND WANTS

Life has taught me
that my needs
—over and over—
are always met.

I always have
food, shelter, clothes.

Life has also taught me
that my wants
—over and over—
always get me in trouble.

**What are you grateful for?**

# The Attitude is Gratitude

When I'm down—depressed, feeling sorry for my-self, I force myself to make a list of all the things I can be grateful for at that moment.

1. Thank you for being alive.
2. Thanks for my family.
3. Thanks for my health today.
4. Thank you for my bed, the shirt on my back, shoes on my feet, my cats, the sunny day, the rainy day, etc.

By the time the list has eight or nine "gratitudes" on it, I realize I'm feeling better. As I continue the list, I feel a lot better.

When I'm not grateful, I'm not happy.

## ON SELF IMPORTANCE

**Life would be
terrific if people
would just realize
who I think I am!**

**Humility brings teachability**

# Willingness Brings Joy

*An amazing discovery for me was the realization that all I had to do was one thing at a time. Sometimes I get very upset when God doesn't do what I want Him to, when I want Him to do it—which must mean He . . . is a She.*

Chill . . . I'm only kidding.

Actually, I'm only kidding about the "She" part of that statement. The other part, of wanting what I want, when I want it and getting upset when it doesn't happen, many times is the truth.

You know what it's like praying so hard to God that you just had to have that mate, job, vacation, car, whatever. Or the big one, the big prayer—dear God please get me out of this and I promise I'll never, ever do it again.

What happens when it doesn't happen and you don't get what you want and God doesn't do what we want?

Anger, resentment, self pity, doubt—those "see, I knew I couldn't count on you"—feelings? Oh, add ego, big time ego, one last attempt at manipulating God with guilt.

Manipulate God? Are you crazy? Such insanity mere mortals toy with, yet I know people who try every day.

I want to do different things, I thought one day. But to do that, I have to learn to do things differently.

The journey has been an interesting, exciting, and wonderful one. It's also been challenging, painful and very difficult at times. Looking back, I really didn't know why I needed to change until I wanted to change.

Willingness, a 100% committed willingness, to face whatever comes—fear, test of faith, bad times, good times—is absolutely the most important part of change.

It used to be severe pain that brought about the willingness to change. When I was doing something that hurt me—and hurt me hard and long enough that I wanted it to stop—then I'd think about changing the way I was. No more.

Thank God for the gift of choice. Today it just takes a little pain to get my attention, for me to take a hard look at why I'm feeling uncomfortable. It's usually because I'm feeling some kind of fear.

Choice is what I have when I acknowledge the fear. With the power of choices I allow faith and hope. Faith and hope eliminate fear.

It's generally only when the pain has me so uncomfortable that I can't find relief that I look at the problem.

To get there means looking in the mirror and being completely honest.

No matter what is happening that is upsetting me, hurting me, making my life less than joyful, the problem is me. It's not the boss, the wife, the IRS, the guy in the car in front. It's me. When I accept that 100% and believe it completely, I've taken the first huge step toward feeling a lot better. When I am honest with me about me, I start to free myself from what's making me unhappy.

Simple, huh? Maybe for some people, but for me, at times the original doubting Thomas, I need to see the results.

&

The ABC's to help you celebrate Life. When you're not happy and peaceful remember:

1. **A**ccept what is happening to you at that moment. Stop resisting. Know that what's happening will change—things always do.

2. **B**elieve that what's happening is for your own good. This proactive thinking helps offset self pity, depression and anger.

3. **C**hoose to think differently. Think proactively instead of reactively; remember reactive thinking is usually based on old, unhealthy pictures.

4. **D**rama—try to lighten up and take the drama out of the situation.

5. **E**vidence—try to identify the cause of your discomfort or unhappiness. Remember you are the problem and you can fix *you*. If you are having difficulty identifying the cause, don't forget that 9 out of 10 times you are unhappy, fear has caused it.

6. **F**ear causes most problems. When fear knocks, answer with Faith.

7. **G**ratitude—be grateful in all ways (always) for what you have at that moment. Gratitude is power.

   It's easy to remember. Just think "A" through "G."

# Solutions—One More Look

Thinking about what I've learned over the years, I believe the most important lesson was how to identify fear and identify it quickly. Whenever I am out of sorts, not happy, restless, irritable, discontent, if I think fear, I am a step closer to identifying what is causing the problem.

A reminder. We all want what we want—to deny that would be dishonest. If there is any doubt that we won't get what we want, it causes fear.

The solution is to bring faith into play immediately. Faith in a power greater then me—for me it's God. When I truly believe and feel that I'm going to be all right, the fear eases and I can focus on the exact nature of what's bothering me.

By that I mean when somebody does something to me and I get upset and stay upset then I am the problem—not the other person. For example: Someone cuts me off on the freeway. He or she is a jerk, that's a given. Getting angry for a short time is natural.

If, ten miles down the road, I am still angry, still wanting to run that idiot off the road, crash into his car, set it on fire, teach him a lesson—then I am the problem. The anger is now resentment (remember *Traffic problems—food for the soul*).

In all cases, when I am not happy, I always turn to choice—a most powerful tool.

I can choose to hit the GAS.

Gratitude—for whatever it is that's happening to me at that moment.

Acceptance—instead of resistance, for acceptance is the key to my serenity.

Surrender—my resistance and choose to believe all that happens is for my good.

Oh, one more thing. I remember that life's a joke and when I get too serious I remind myself that God wants me to be happy. About the only thing not funny about life is death and there's nothing I can do about that but accept it . . . and hope I'm not there when it comes.

I'm here to tell you change doesn't come easy, but as you change, life gets easier.

෴

# The Stallion and the Long Run

*I have been running hard, full out into the wind for many days and many nights. Deep in the darkness of the desert, exhausted, I stumble, but do not fall for this—this is my long run.*

The night breeze chills the sweat on my body. Moonbeams bounce off my shining coat of black and white. And I think.

For years my life was black and white, wrong or right. Today, this night, I am a stallion that no longer believes life is just black or white, wrong or right. I raise my head higher, proud, and I smile, for no longer do I need to hide behind being right.

The full hunters' moon calls to me; rest, it says, it is time to rest; yet possessed, I run until I fall. Ah, old ways die hard.

Lying there, a feeling of peace comes over me. A coyote howls—another answers.

Looking up, deep into the universe, the heavens and 10 zillion stars stare back—I am thankful—thankful for life's many gifts.

The moon to light my way in the darkness.

*Courage* to confront fear—to fight despair.

*Humility* to teach me to bend, to yield, to learn to change.

*Acceptance* of what is and what I cannot change.

*Wisdom* to walk away from having to be right, to know the difference whether to stand and fight.

Winds of *Change* to blow away false pride; winds bringing happiness instead of righteousness. Winds that bring serenity.

Peaceful, content, I fall asleep.

Dawn's first light brings a gentle breeze, and with it, the sweet smell of renewed life. It is water, and it is nearby.

Quickly lifting my head, sniffing the air, I'm still for just a moment, listening, inhaling deeply, trusting the wind will show me the way to water.

Thank you, Great Spirit, thank you. Breathing deeply, feeling the power, the peace, I lay my head back down, resting, thinking.

The winds of change have brought me home—home to myself. The winds of change have given me understanding of who I am, and, lovingly, I have accepted *me*.

Turning to the east, half a sun peeks from behind the mountain. It is reaching, climbing into a pale blue sky, its loving rays stretch into the cool desert warming me, pushing the chill of the night further west.

I close my eyes, a bird sings . . . a shadow crosses my light. I open my eyes and see the arms of a giant saguaro cactus raised in prayer in dawn's early light.

"Thank you, Great Spirit, for a new day," I hear it say.

I stir and stretch and yawn and, as I do, the blooming desert flowers—red and yellow, orange and purple—brushing my belly, tickling me, teasing me, tempting me to play.

Filled with renewed strength, I rise. Muscles aching, I move slowly but steadily to the water hole. A quick smell brings joy, a deep drink brings a grateful heart for the gift so secret in the desert.

The sweet smell of sacred sage is in the air and the perfume of my life brings a sense of peace; I am renewed—I am whole.

It has been a long run and I still stand. I have survived the wounds of life, of lessons learned, of heartbreak and sorrow.

Shaking my head, I celebrate, joyfully kissing the wind. Turning my face full to the sun and I am ready—ready to run again, to play, to dance across the desert floor, for no longer do I run against the wind. No longer in my life is there running from—now, it is all running to, for today, I run with the wind.

ᘜ

**Autumn, 1997**

**Just back from a walk . . .**

**There is a part of me
on a cool autumn morning,
when geese cry
and rise majestically
in front of me,
that still makes me go
Boom! Boom!**

**The hunter still stirs,
but the warrior is at ease.**

# THE SERENITY PRAYER

**God
grant me
the serenity
to accept
the things
I cannot change,
the courage
to change
the things I can,
and the wisdom
to know
the difference.**

**Reinhold Niebuhr**

# Give Yourself Credit

It's the hard, fearless, work you do that brings about change. Recognize, respect and give yourself the credit you deserve when you have the courage to change your life. Shamelessly, with healthy pride, when you make progress celebrate it.

Remember, it's progress that brings joy, not perfection.

If you'd like to share your thoughts, comments, questions or stories you can reach me at:

Jerry Stanecki Productions, Inc.
P.O. Box 121
Bloomfield Hills, MI  48303
or e-mail: stanecki@wwnet.net
www.jerrystanecki.com


And remember, when you get it—give it away.
You will feel wonderful.
Warmest regards,

*Jerry Stanecki*

| Item | Price | S & H |
|------|-------|-------|
| Life is a Joke and God Wrote It | $14.95 | $3.55 |

**AUDIO TAPES**

| | | |
|------|-------|-------|
| An Evening with Jerry Stanecki<br>An hour of talk and life stories as Jerry reads<br>some of his columns. | $10.00 | $2.00 |
| Lighten Up—Enjoy the Journey<br>Learn about the power of play and laughing<br>instead of crying. | $7.00 | $2.00 |
| Hoffa—The Last Interview<br>An hour-long tape of Jerry interviewing Jimmy Hoffa<br>for *Playboy Magazine*. This remarkable piece of<br>history is still shrouded with the mystery of<br>"What happened to Jimmy Hoffa." | $5.00 | $2.00 |

QUANTITY DISCOUNTS ARE AVAILABLE

MICHIGAN RESIDENTS, PLEASE INCLUDE 6% SALES TAX

To order any of the above items, please send a check or money order to:

**Spirit Canyon Press**
**P. O. Box 121**
**Bloomfield Hills, MI 48303**

Please allow a reasonable time for delivery

For more information, comments, columns and e-mail please go to:

**www.jerrystanecki.com**